I0531698

PART ONE: YOU IN THE EQUATION

BANG

HEAD

HERE

A GUIDE TO RECONNECTION, COMMUNICATION, AND COACHING OUR LOVED ONES

JOSH BRAZIER & HOLLIE HENDERSON

ISBN 979-8-9853815-0-4

Portions of this book are works of nonfiction. Certain names and identifying characteristics have been changed.

Front cover design by Heidi Helm.
Book design by Hannah Rushton.
Editing by Hannah Rushton and Kara Matsuda.

Printed in the United States of America.

First Printing, 2022.

Ally Publishing
Las Vegas, Nevada

www.JoshandHollie.com

We are grateful to be your connection ally.

Contents

PREFACE

Does your head hurt?

We know how it feels to continually bang your head against the wall because we've been there; when those we coached struggled to change their destructive behaviors, we couldn't help but bang our heads against the wall. It's painful, frustrating, and uncertain, isn't it?

We know there are limited resources to help you navigate what you're going through. It's frustrating not knowing what to do next. Because of that we felt inspired to write *Bang Head Here*. We knew we could help.

We've been coaching teens and adults for over a decade who have dealt with drug and alcohol addictions, eating disorders, personality disorders, sexual and family violence, neglect, learning disabilities, and challenging home environments. We've had to overcome our own addictions and self-destruct patterns similarly. We know what works—and what doesn't work or makes things worse.

This is not a book of easy fixes. You will learn to see yourself and your loved ones differently, accept things and people differently, and work through the discomfort differently. You will practice new ways of talking and relating, and try on different approaches and ideas. You and your loved ones will make mistakes in this process. But, don't worry, it's normal. Forgive each other and move on.

But, don't forget: we are your ally. You are not alone while you explore, question, and change. If you are ready, we're ready!

All names, other than the authors' names, have been changed for privacy.

INTRODUCTION
by Josh Brazier

In a remote part of southwest India, I found myself in a dormitory filled with exhausted volunteers and boys currently enrolled in my residence-based treatment center. I was having a really good conversation with a boy from northern California, Ethan[1], who I had really connected to at the center. Insanely intelligent and head strong, he found drugs early in life and never looked back.

Out of nowhere, the humid clouds burst and we were stuck indoors in the middle of a hot Indian monsoon. On a whim, Ethan and I decided to take our conversation outside. We walked laps around the orphanage property where we were serving for a while. Kids from the orphanage watched us silently from their windows with confused faces, obviously wondering what these two crazy Americans were doing. We were connecting on a deep level and Ethan became really important to me in that moment, someone I would always look after. I had high hopes for Ethan. I imagine all caretakers know this feeling.

Fast forward a few years and Ethan had been kicked out of high school and college his freshman year. I had been there for each up and down, always hoping Ethan's potential would be realized. With each emergency phone call from his parents, I was more and more disappointed.

[1] All names have been changed for privacy.

More time passed. In a last ditch effort to clear Ethan's head, we traveled to Africa with a group to help out on some important projects. The moment we touched down, Ethan was seeking drugs from every pharmacy, feigning back problems to get drugs from doctors. It was exhausting. Taking a group to Africa is exhausting enough, so dealing with a drug-seeking volunteer drove me to the edge.

I finally lost it on Ethan, yelling and screaming at him in a van full of volunteers. I scared myself and some of the volunteers. The last bits of our connection on that rainy night in India had worn off. Everything was raw, it was scary, and I felt helpless with Ethan for the first time in my life. I felt the same kind of desperation that I had heard in the voices of many parents. Maybe for the first time, I empathized with my clients and their parents. I understood what "at wit's end" really meant.

Ethan and I lost touch after Africa until I found him on the streets of Santa Cruz after a desperate morning-long search to find him. He was high and as we sat down to a meal, he couldn't keep his eyes open. He begged for money, for a hotel room. He was grasping for some stability and I so badly wanted to rescue him. As I left him with some friends at a shady motel off the boardwalk in Santa Cruz, I wondered if I would ever see Ethan again. My heart ached the whole way back to LA and my face was as wet as that night in India. Had we lost Ethan?

Ethan went in and out of jail for the next year or so. I would get updates from his parents and they were never good.

Ethan had finally hit his rock bottom during his last stint in jail and he and his parents decided on an alternative form of treatment for him out of country. We had a week before the center could receive him and we just had to get him there before he wandered back to his old life. On my flight to go pick him up in San Francisco, I wondered if Ethan and I would ever connect like we did in India, and if all this effort I was about to expend would be worth it. I quietly promised myself to start fresh: my only goal was to get Ethan to Mexico for treatment.

What followed was a week of me playing mentor, drug dealer, and caretaker. It was hellish. I stayed up all night, checking his breathing. I ate the food Ethan had learned to make while incarcerated. We drove all over California trying to keep him calm and just high enough to prevent him from wandering off.

After I dropped him off in Mexico, I reflected on what I expected. Were my attempts to reconnect and rebuild our relationship going to be successful, or would we go back to where we started? I let Ethan go with a slim hope, trying to let go of my attachment to his outcome.

Days later, I received a call.

"Josh?"

"Ethan? Is that you?"

It was the old Ethan's voice I knew so well, clear and calm, and free from addiction.

"Thank you."

It's the only thing I remember him saying to me. I felt that we were back on our road to reconnection. He was finally free from his addictions, and ready to start anew in his life. Today, years later, he is still drug free and thriving.

Just like Ethan and many others we've worked with, there is hope for you and your loved ones. We know the struggle is heart-wrenching at times. We know this journey is a process. The process with Ethan took four years of going from awesome, to awful, and then back to better. You may be going through the exact same thing, or something wildly different. Whatever concerns or fears you have, today is the day for self discovery, growth, and renewal. This book will be the start of your road to reconnection with someone. It will help you overcome your current struggles with your loved one.

We are happy to journey with you. We applaud you for looking at yourself and your relationships in a new way—a way that might be painful initially, but will inevitably help you grow. It is our greatest hope that the principles and stratagems we have developed and used with clients over the last ten years will bring your loved ones closer to you and allow for deeper connection, bonding, and love.

Please take into account that even though the stories we relay may have nothing to do with your current reality, the simple principles about connection, healthy communication, and coaching can be adapted to what you are experiencing. We have found that because people are so different, there is rarely one path to successful connection. However, we believe there are certain core principles and stratagems that can produce better results—when used consistently and correctly with loved ones.

We have also found that when you remain flexible within the framework of these core principles, you can better meet the needs of others. Being flexible has been vital to our success because it allows us the space to grow and to discover our clients and their individual needs. Just like people, not every cake has the same ingredients, but the core of the cake is the same. The variation depends on the cake maker and or the cake eater. The same analogy can be used with those we love. We all need connection, acceptance, support, and unconditional love to thrive, but some of us may need one-on-one time, as opposed to others who seek adventure and activities that allow them to socialize. You have to discover whatever your loved one needs to be their best. You just need to be flexible along the way while you work with your recipe.

NOTE

As you continue to read, please note that the scope of traditional families has shifted over the past twenty years to more single parent homes, grandparents, aunts, and uncles raising children, foster parents, godparents, mentors, step parents, and more. With the hopes of making this process as relevant as possible for you and your family, we will refer to any person caring for an individual as *the caretaker* and to the one receiving the care as *the loved one*, rather than mom, dad, child, teenager, or young adult.

One

IT STARTS WITH YOU

Faced with the choice between changing one's mind and proving that there is no need to do so, almost everyone gets busy on the proof.

—John Kenneth Galbraith

We would rather be ruined than changed; We would rather die in our dread Than climb the cross of the moment And let our illusions die.

—W.H. Auden

Several years ago during a lunch meeting, we found ourselves delving into the minute nuances of what heals a disconnect between loved ones. It was a fascinating discussion, and one that led us to mutually agree that when connection is lost, the damage cannot be repaired on the shoulders of one.

Up until that point, much of our coaching efforts had been focused on people who were at risk, spending hours unraveling their conflicts and issues only to return them to the exact environment that allowed their dysfunction and disconnect to grow. We found ourselves frustrated—banging our heads against a wall—more than we wanted to when things would go so wrong, especially after they had gone so well. Until we learned that we had to change their environment in addition to their attitude, a lot of our efforts were lost because of an unhealthy environment. Not only did we have to continue teaching the at-risk loved one healthy tools for personal regulation, but we also had to start with the caretaker. We had to change the way the caretaker related and interacted with their loved one.

He was doing great, really making friends with others at the center. I was really proud of him. He was on his way to fulfilling some dreams and some goals we'd talked about. I never imagined I'd get a call six months later from his mom telling me he was right back to where they started. After talking to him, I put the pieces together real fast. He had changed, but mom had not.

—Robbie

I lived away from home during a time of rehabilitation. For the first time in my life, I felt I was coming into my own, that I had a space to breathe and feel like myself. Nobody was there to criticize my thoughts. I no longer felt like I was constantly in trouble, or in the hot seat. I started to come alive. Then I heard my caretakers were coming to town to visit, and to work with my counselor. I was terrified. Would this all go away, my newfound freedom, when they arrived? I couldn't sleep. I found myself going on bike rides to escape. I found myself shutting down. In counseling, it was awful! It felt like nothing had changed, that we were stuck. They kept blaming me, talking over me, hurting me. I wanted to run away. It wasn't until later sessions that they finally realized I wasn't going to survive if we didn't change together.

—Celeste

So it starts with the caretaker.

You may be thinking, "What do you mean it starts with me? I'm not the problem here. My loved one is the one who clearly needs help. Help them, and leave me alone."

We know a crisis with a loved one is not all about the caretaker. We know it may be difficult, feeling paralyzed and at a loss about what to do to help them. We also know that you as the caretaker are doing the very best you know. We aren't trying to blame you. But what we do know, after years of coaching, is that whenever you are disconnected from a loved one, it will add to the crisis. You both have to change.

So, we start with you because you are most likely the parent figure. As a parent figure and caretaker, you are so much more important than you know. It's easy to lose sight of that truth after years of care-taking and often years of feeling unappreciated by a loved one. But even today, regardless of the hurt or loss you have suffered with your loved one, your loved one is aching to reconnect with you. When loved ones don't feel connected, they can become easily distracted by things to fill that void. Typically, these void-filling activities are troublesome. When loved ones are left to decide how to fill the void, they typically choose dangerous and harmful activities. In the end, your connection to your

loved one is incredibly vital to their emotional stability and their healing process.

A few months ago, I remember sitting in session with a gentlemen in his
mid-forties who had decided to make a career switch and was looking for
some one-on-one coaching to help him with some personal obstacles. In
his younger years, he witnessed violence perpetuated by his father towards
his mother, and witnessed his mother's traumatic attempted suicides. I
understood why his relationships were getting in the way of his success.
He felt deeply committed to never being the bad man his caretaker was.
With these feelings, he became the opposite to the extreme, always looking
to protect the women around him even if he needed to sacrifice his own
feelings and needs. This was starting to take a toll on his personal and professional life.

During our session, after years of pent-up emotion, he finally began to
cry as he said, "I have tried to have a relationship with my dad and show
him that I am a good man. I am the only one of all of his kids that has
ever done something with his life. I'm the only one that ever finished high
school and is pursuing further education." His sorrow deepened as he said,
"I just want my father to tell me that he is proud of me . . . I want to feel like
he approves of me."

This was a heartbreaking moment for me to see this man so distraught
over a broken connection that he felt he needed. He wanted to bond with
his father so deeply that he blinded himself from reality. The man he craved
acceptance from was a dad who terrorized his family through physical and
mental violence, as well as personal neglect. This man had waited 40 years
to feel connected, accepted, and validated; he is, like many people, starving
for connection.

Caretakers leave an incredibly powerful imprint on the lives of their
loved ones, for good or bad. Caretakers are irreplaceable. To help a struggling loved one, you have to create a new awareness and reality that every
moment counts. Things that you say and do, ways you react or don't react,
and anything you do counts in the life of your loved one, and could be
adding to their current crisis in a negative way.

If you are not completely satisfied with the connection you have with
any loved one, take a moment to ask yourself: "How am I missing opportunities to connect, communicate, and coach those that matter most in
my life?"

Quite often, the most painful reality is to accept when things aren't going right in your relationship—that it is your own personal involvement
that is creating a disconnection. You might be creating some of what

you are experiencing. This game of connection cannot be played with one person; it takes multiple people actively moving forward together towards a win.

Today, we'd like to move forward with you. If you want a relationship with your loved one, and if your loved one is struggling with addictions or other healthy relationship obstacles, you will first need to make sure your relationship and connection with them is solid. This may not completely solve your problems, but their ability to bounce back and heal will be much easier if they can rely on a relationship that adds air to their sails, rather than leaving them in stagnant waters.

When we started asking caretakers to accept this idea of being actively involved in their loved ones recovery, they would often push back. Here is an example of one such caretaker:

> It was really difficult at first wrapping my mind around the idea that I was part of the equation. I felt my loved one was the one making all the mistakes and I was the one stuck dealing with the fall out, stuff I never wanted to deal with. It wasn't my fault they were lying to me and doing things behind my back. It wasn't my fault they were getting caught in the process. They were hurting me, and I was the one really suffering here. So, when I was asked to take a look at myself in the equation, I was really bothered by that. Then I started to realize below the surface there was much more going on—stuff I hadn't even considered—that was driving a wedge between my loved one and I. This is when I started to understand that changing didn't mean I was wrong or a bad parent, it just meant that we needed to do something different to connect again.
>
> —Chelsea

When our clients were able to drop their sword and face their opponent with the intent to connect, it wasn't about who was right or wrong anymore, who hurt who, or who needed to change. It was about figuring out how to come together again. The power in changing themselves and their mindset also quickly disarmed their loved ones, putting them in a much better place for discovery and reconnection. This change provided a completely different landscape for possible healing.

When you are stuck in the same rut, banging your head against the same wall, this means you're probably not going anywhere different. If you can be flexible to change, continually checking in with your relationship, and willing to shift as they shift, you can succeed in the game of connection. It all starts with your willingness to let go and start anew.

For example, this loved one noticed the exact moment his caretakers started using this method.

> The most powerful moment in our transformation was when I noticed my caretakers making the first effort to accept responsibility to show they wanted to change. It softened me. I had become so defensive and hard from all of our issues. This was the moment I felt hope, and that my life might actually be worth living.
>
> —Joshua

If you are feeling uneasy about changing, we invite you to let go. At this point, you have nothing to lose and only incredible insights ahead to gain. It will take courage to look at yourself and your relationships in different ways, to become more self aware of your actions or inactions during those troubling times, and to learn how you can change the tide in the future. We know you can do it.

Always keep in mind what you really want to accomplish: to help your loved one heal and to build a relationship with them. If that means you have to put aside everything you thought you knew to do so, do it. Start today by saying, "If I want things to change, I must be prepared to change myself."

REFLECTIVE POINTS & CORE PRINCIPLES TO REMEMBER:

- Do not expect your loved one to do all the work repairing the damage between the two of you just because they are making harmful decisions.

- Let go of the belief that others will be able to solve your conflict problems, and accept that it will take a team of people involved, you being the most important.

- When stuck in a head-banging rut, change yourself and the way you react to your loved one. When you change, you provide a completely different landscape for possible healing. When they see you are willing to engage in a relationship differently, they will be more willing to meet you and change as well.

WE WANT TO HEAD YOU OFF AT THE PASS.

This book is a deep dive into *you* and is not a quick fix. We know that you are probably searching for things to minimize the fights, the drama, the pain, and the hurt. We hear you. As you go through this book and subsequent follow-up books, you might want to know what you can do today to minimize the strain on your relationship. We suggest that you start by "disengaging."

DISENGAGE

First and foremost, learn to disengage. Pride, fear, and your need for control keep you engaged in the fight. Let those emotions go. They haven't served you thus far and it won't in the future. Disengage.

What are some examples of disengaging from the fight?

- When a fight surfaces, don't react like you have in the past. If you yell, manipulate, talk over people, or ignore, STOP!
- Stop pushing your agenda of what you think your loved one might need while you discover more about what's really going on with your loved one.

- If you're scared about the direction your loved one is going, don't add to the issue by becoming overly protective, controlling, and emotional—despite how challenging it may be.

Why? It has become obvious to us as coaches who are *in* the home that many do not recognize when their loved ones are not healthy emotionally. Caretakers continue to engage, prod, and persevere all while their loved one is struggling inside. Nothing good happens when any human being is emotionally unhealthy.

When you continue to push for your agenda while a loved one is in a emotionally unhealthy state, one message is very clear to your loved one: *You* are not listening!

All of this costs your relationship dearly.

So, disengage, breathe, and observe your fear. Become an observer of what's going on inside yourself, but also be an observer of what your loved one looks like when they are emotionally unhealthy. Store all the information away and start to observe and document their patterns and triggers for now. Understanding patterns and triggers will help you in the future to understand when your loved one is struggling.

WHAT CAN I SAY TODAY?

What can you say to your loved one—even while your relationship seems to be in total chaos—to help you gain traction with them?

Guard your words. Make sure that what you say today is lifting and void of judgement. Avoid embarrassing or cutting remarks. If you're normally a sarcastic person and you project that towards your loved one in a negative way, stop. This will not benefit anyone in the long run.

Apologize. Don't be afraid of it. It doesn't mean you're broken or a bad person. It just means you have enough control over your emotions to offer the powerful healing balm that comes from apologizing, regardless of whether you feel that it's justified or not.

When you don't know what to say because you seem to make things worse no matter what, follow this caretaker's example of accepting what she didn't know, expressing it, and sharing her intent to change:

> I didn't really know what to do for my loved one when he started to spiral downward. He was making decisions that terrified me. I wanted to just pull my action plan together about next steps and execute it just

so I could stop the emotional flatline I was in. I wanted to stop the pain I was in, and my fear for his future. I felt justified too because I felt more capable, older, and more prepared. But, every time I would try and do what I thought was best, we would hit rock bottom all over again. I had a hard time leaving any decision in his hands about the future because I felt like he was too far over the edge to manage himself. I felt I needed to intervene or he would be dead. Ultimately, what took the most courage in the end was saying to him, "I know you are hurting. I see you. I want things to get better. I don't have all of the answers today, but I'm ready to listen so we can find the answers together. I'm sorry if I left you emotionally alone and afraid. I want to change this, and the way we are together."

Wow! It is so powerful for a loved one to be seen this way, isn't it? For both parties, this is a journey that nobody expected to take, and there's no road map. Accept that, forgive and apologize when needed, and move forward.

WHAT PHYSICAL ACTIONS SHOULD I TAKE?

What can you physically do to show that you are ready to end the disconnect? Give them your time in a way that is positive and productive. If you're always busy, start this week by setting aside some time to just be with your loved one. Most people think this needs to be a production, like a special night out, but quite often, struggling loved ones would love for you to just listen to their day without picking up your phone and getting distracted. They love it, just like you love feeling unique and special to someone. Sometimes the biggest communicator to those you love that you care is when you connect with them eye to eye and respond to what they are saying with sincere interest. When they tell a story that was crazy to them respond with something like, "Wow, that sounds insane!" Be sure to then follow up with a question that suggests you really want to know more.

Don't expect this to go perfectly, especially when there is a lot of tension. Most importantly, don't allow yourself to react if your time together starts to go south. If it does, wrap things up without reacting and try again later. But please start trying to change the way that you connect. This personalized connection needs to happen in some form or another at least once a day. If you can help them feel loved and valued at least once a day, you'll have a great start. Here are some ways you can do that:

- Show appreciation for the way they helped you when they had other things to do, even when they grumbled about it.

- Send them a text. Sure you could send "I love you," if you felt this is what they need and it feels appropriate, but sometimes just a funny text or joke or photo that makes them know you care or are thinking about them is great. However, don't send these messages after you had a disagreement. This feels disingenuous and forced. To a loved one, it feels like you are just sending these messages so you can feel good about what just happened, especially when things are left unresolved.
- Leave them a surprise note somewhere.
- Catch them in the act of doing something nice for someone and build them up with a genuine compliment: "It's amazing how you connect with people, you're so good at that."

We know its hard to connect when you might have frustrated feelings towards a loved one. But, someone has to lead if both parties feel the same, and this needs to be you.

WHAT ABOUT PHYSICAL CONTACT?

If a loved one is in a moment of emotional unhealthiness, and they have feelings of aggression towards you, our guess is that this type of affection within your family is long gone or minimally expressed. This doesn't mean that they or you don't want that connection, it just means that it isn't safe yet. Don't try and force a hug or some type of connection because it makes you feel better about what's going on. However, if there is a moment that you feel like the person would be receptive, you can try.

Sometimes words aren't enough. Being embraced, especially after a difficult fight in which everyone feels resolved, creates an opportunity to bond and connect. If the exchange is mutual and authentic, it is more powerful than just a verbal exchange.

I've had fights before when I felt like we said all was good, and then we just went into separate rooms and did our own thing, which really didn't make me feel very connected to that person. The relationships that made me feel the most secure after an argument were the ones where the person who I was angry with, after we resolved our issues came up and gave me a hug, or I hugged them. When it was a hug with an accompanied "I'm sorry", I just felt like that person meant it even more, and that they wanted to be close to me. It made it easier to forgive and move on."

— Andi

HOW DO I LET GO OF MY PAIN?

How do you let go of your pain and concern so you can better connect with your loved one?

> It's hard to love my son right now after everything he's been doing. I catch him in so many lies, and he won't even say sorry. It's hard for me to be nice to him because I'm so angry.

—Erin

Even though you may be angry, in this moment what your loved one needs the most is understanding, empathy, and support, or their cycle will continue to deepen. We aren't talking about condoning behavior, but about burying your anger to prevent making things worse. So, how do you pull yourself together so that you don't project anger?

Take breaks—lots and lots of breaks if necessary. When anger floods in, excuse yourself until you can contain it.

Don't approach your loved one if you are feeling angry and reactive, it will *never* help!

Try to create opportunities to connect that have nothing to do with drama, so you can be reminded of why you love your loved one.

Try and laugh more with this loved one. Remember that even in the darkest night of the soul, the day does come. Be the laughter that brings in the new light.

When you don't feel any joy, take some time to connect with the things that make you smile, like watching funny videos, listening to a good joke, connecting with a friend. Focus on the little things that help to swing pain into hope.

One of the best ways to deal with anger is to acknowledge your own imperfections. When you are angry at your loved one, take a moment to honor that you too have made mistakes that have made others angry. Ask yourself, "Is it fair how I react to this person when I have been guilty of doing the same thing in some other way or form? How would I have wanted someone to deal with me?" Let your answer be your guide.

THE WRAP UP

If there's one word we want you to walk away with today—you guessed it—it's *disengage*. Disengage, for now! Disengage until you learn how to connect in a healthier way as you read through each chapter. Disengage not only from fights with loved ones, but from all the negative habits, patterns, and stories that have led you to this point. Instead, it is *you* that is becoming more focused, willing to figure this dissociation out.

Just remember, It will get better, if you decide to get better.

Two

THE BREAKDOWN

"Breakdowns are breakthroughs. Sometimes it takes hitting the bottom to find your way to the top."

—Unknown

You may or may not be aware that breakdowns don't happen in a week, a month, or even a couple months. They tend to happen over an extended period of time. Breakdowns happen when loved ones experience pain or trauma and don't know how to deal with it. It's progressive: a breakdown could start with a major event, followed by a collection of smaller thoughts and validating moments that feed into this experience. It could also be a series of smaller moments spread out over an extended period of time that create so much discomfort over time that loved ones cannot cope.

During my teenage years, my parents and I had a rough go at it. I can't tell you an exact weekend or date things started to tank, but I can tell you about exact moments, how I felt, how things were resolved, and how I started to move further away from my family.

—Hannah

I started to break down when I was thirteen. It probably took about a year from the time all those bad moments started to add up in my head that led to a break down. I didn't let anyone know how I was feeling during that whole year. On the outside things seemed fine, but on the inside, I was not well. Once I hit my breaking point, it took about two months before my parents realized what was going on.

—Madeline

"I never had a visible breakdown. My breakdown occurred on a personal level well into my adult years. Sure as a teen I would get in trouble, but it all seemed very benign to the outsider. I was stressed. I had an image to uphold that I perceived was given to me by my family and those around me. I couldn't let them down, and I couldn't let myself down. So I created perfection in the eyes of others and lived a double life exploring and delving into things that would disrupt my image, but I felt I needed to explore. It crashed down one day for me in my early adult years and I have been letting people down ever since. My story may seem strange, but it is typical for those who live under a roof of crippling expectations and unrealistic demands from family and community."

—Adam

We often don't think that how *we* resolve conflict adds to our loved ones' breakdowns, but we should. When we look at Adam's story, his symptoms seemed unnoticeable on the surface; no huge arguments or any outward appearance of problems at home. When asked about his relationship with his caretakers, he's quick to admit there was no relationship. We later found that his caretakers admitted to fitting into the "Passive Dad, Anxious Mom" default patterns we talk about in Chapter 5, which left Brandon feeling more disconnected.

It seems almost too simple to state that healthy relationship building within families requires an all-hands-on-deck approach. Placing total blame on the person who is struggling rarely solves the problem. However, acknowledging how, why, and where we need to shift in order to build relationships that are more positive, and then actually making the effort consistently to change is not simple.

SECRET WORLD = SAFER ME

I got to a point where I would just tell my parents what I knew they wanted to hear just because I didn't want to deal with the fighting, or because I felt like they would never accept me if I told them what I really felt. Secretly inside, I was so sad. I just felt like I wanted to cry all the time and felt that nobody really cared.

—Shalene

Loved ones who are starting to breakdown have complicated thoughts, beliefs, and are conflicted internally. What they once believed about themselves internally is challenged externally by what they are experiencing around them at school, at home, at church, with friends, or with strangers. Who they want to be is possibly being squashed, and who they are being forced to become might be unbearable. The day-to-day complications of living life has become overwhelming for them, especially when they haven't felt like anyone truly understands their feelings or knows how to support those feelings.

They may also be afraid to open up in fear that they might disappoint those they feel connected to. This place of refuge inside their head may be the only safe place they have to help them deal with the outside world. Even more complicated is the duality they create, the two different people they've formed in their heads—one person that deeply struggles, and the other who seems to be fine. When they decide to use this duality to navigate their relationships, things become even more complex. This is when parents and loved ones become confused or feel lied to. The loved one is so good at hiding their feelings and acting the part of the old self—especially when they feel highly threatened—that they are okay feeling unsafe instead of showing who they really feel they are or who they are becoming.

> I wanted to be the good kid my parents thought I was and at times it was easy to. But deep down, that kid wasn't liked at school. That kid was made fun of, and even though my parents talked about being a leader and standing for what I believed, I never felt like I could do that by myself. I needed to belong, and if belonging meant I had to give up some things I knew I shouldn't do … well, that was less painful than being alone. So I had to be careful about when I did things and what I talked about with my parents. I didn't want my life to change, because I was finally making friends."
>
> —Derrick

You might be thinking, "Are you saying I don't know my own kid?" Yes, you might not know your own loved one *if* your loved one senses in anyway that they could disappoint you, be rejected by you, or feel any negative backlash. If they know you wouldn't be comfortable with what's going on in their lives, they will retreat into a safe space and most likely hide who they are becoming. Often, this real self is very different than the person you think you've been dealing with.

It's a scary thought for someone to realize that they have been making decisions and reacting to someone who they don't really know. A caretaker may only get authentic glimpses here or there. It's scary because what you thought was true and real no longer exists, and what you are doing may not be working. *Even worse, what you are doing could be further damaging your loved one.*

Take a moment to let that sink in. It's not that you're necessarily a bad caretaker, it's that you've just been trying to make chocolate cake for a loved one who actually likes strawberry and you never knew it.

Knowing this changes everything, doesn't it? As you ask yourself these question, you should start to feel the shift of blame release:

- While I was busy trying to do my best with and for my loved one, what did I miss?
- What did I assume?
- How did my need to have things peaceful in the house—to keep things happy—keep me from truly being there for my loved one?
- What does my loved one really think about life?
- How do they feel about themselves?
- What things could they be experiencing that are incredibly hard and stressful for them?

I know my mom wanted the best for us, but the constant diet she had put me on, and the way she would question and watch everything I ate made me feel shameful about myself. I didn't say anything about it because I didn't want anyone to know I felt that way. I mean I was pudgy, so it must be my fault, though it made me hate myself more. I was ashamed that I felt fat. How do you talk about that when you are a young girl who doesn't feel like you have a voice? She didn't know that I hurt deep inside from the rejection I felt around me, and how I felt that everyone was annoyed by me. So, when I started losing weight on my own and people started to notice me in a positive way, I became terrified of losing that attention because it felt so good. Sometimes I wonder if we had just both talked about what wasn't going well, without me feeling the fear of it coming back to bite me, if I might have opened up a bit more. But she was the boss, and I was her little girl. I couldn't tell her she was doing anything wrong because that would have made things worse, and I didn't need worse.

—Kaitlin

We suspect this mom had the best intentions for her daughter, and was concerned about her daughter's future regarding her weight. The approach she took when communicating her hidden fears squashed her daughter, which made Kaitlin feel shameful and defeated. This led Kaitlin to secretly breakdown inside and develop an eating disorder to cope with the turmoil she felt. It wasn't until Mom started to take some ownership about her part in the breakdown that they were able to correct some behaviors and move forward to better connectivity.

HOW DO I PREVENT THE BREAKDOWN?

We want to protect ourselves from pain and discomfort. It is human nature. So, we either quickly solve problems or we place the responsibility on someone else to quickly solve it for us. Therefore, it's natural to be concerned with this question in regards to a loved one.

But, there may be an even better question to ask: "What can I do to build a stronger relationship with my loved one so that when she starts to struggle, I am connected enough to help her solve her conflict?"

We want you to ask this question because, regardless of the warning signs we'll talk about in the next pages that signal a breakdown, we can often miss those signs because we're caught up in our own lives and our own responsibilities. It is much more useful to devote time to building a relationship that can deal with future challenges than getting too caught up in trying to prevent and control future outcomes. You cannot foresee how your loved one could possibly have a major breakdown.

Since people are unique and there is no sure way of avoiding major breakdowns for everyone, you will need to do the best you can to create an environment that is safe for conversation, build your relationships in a positive way, and pay attention to your intuition—it can guide you to see things you may not have seen before. You will find greater success taking this approach than allowing your anxiety to drive you towards false assumptions because that will hurt you and your loved one more. Success begins with being truly connected in a positive way. Then and only then are you in a greater position to notice and reverse the direction your loved one is traveling before they reach rock bottom.

With that being said, let's talk about signs of breakdowns from our experience that may help you recognize when things are shifting poorly for your loved one. Even though we mentioned everyone is different in how they breakdown, these signs are consistently seen with those we've coached.

SIGNALS OF A FUTURE BREAKDOWN

If your loved one starts to behave in these ways, these behaviors could signal a future breakdown:

- They start to become increasingly silent and detached, wanting to spend most of their time alone or away from the family.

- When disagreements occur, they argue and then quickly shut down when they realize they are not being understood or heard. This can become a repeated cycle where they disconnect further and further each time, and engage less and less.

- Their behaviors, dress, and overall appearance starts to change.

- They feel that nobody likes them and that things are always unfair.

- They are overly secretive with their phone, email, notebook, or laptop. (This is not to be confused with the natural desire for space as loved ones mature.) This is the sort of person who goes to great lengths to hide and protect any incoming messages.

- They seem out of sorts and very unhappy. The world is not good in their eyes. You find them moping and often alone, with no desire to call anyone or get involved in doing things with other people.

- They put on an over-the-top show that things are perfect, and that nothing ever goes wrong. (This is not to be confused with the loved one that was born with a natural positive outlook on life.) This can be someone that appears to be putting on a show because they are afraid to show their true feelings, or because they are trying to distract you from other things they are involved with.

- They are always at odds with you and other family members.

- They go dark (meaning they disappear and you can't locate them). When they finally tell you where they've been and what they've been doing, the stories seem a bit odd or trigger your gut that something is off.

- You find them lying quite a bit and feel like you are sometimes dealing with someone who has a split personality.

- They become obsessed with certain things like video games, becoming a pop star, appearances, shopping, or the like. When pulled or kept from their obsessions, they become angry and volatile.

- They start defending their friends over their loved ones, making concessions for them, and show that their loyalty lies elsewhere.

- They are constantly changing their mind to fit whatever circumstance they are in. This displays a real lack of self-esteem and the need for validation internally where they might be struggling with self image.

- They act as if they could care less about you or anyone around them. They become in-sensitive and arrogant.

- When the company they keep is problematic, it is a sure sign of future problems to come.

- They are very co-dependent on a girlfriend or boyfriend. Their insecurities have them seeking out companions that would validate them, but also possibly abuse them and set them up for further failure and breakdown.

I'm sure you can come up with quite a few other warning signs you've experienced with your loved one that we haven't mentioned. When you start to notice shifts, we ask that you don't react by jumping to conclusions, as that could add more damage to your situation. Do think about how to approach your loved one in conversation with hopes to uncover the problem—this is even more important than their negative behaviors. You want to get to the root of their current beliefs or how they feel about their lives—and also how you might be adding to that stress.

Deep pain is at the root of all breakdowns, as well as the inability to cope with that pain. If you truly want to help your loved ones out of destructive cycles, you will need to understand how a loss of connection creates pain, which can trigger breakdowns, which can then lead to addiction. In Chapter 3, we will have you take a deeper look at your loved ones journey with pain as well as your own. Until then, take a moment to sit with these reflective points:

REFLECTIVE POINTS & CORE PRINCIPLES TO REMEMBER:

- A breakdown doesn't happen overnight. It's a process that happens over time, either from personal trauma or loss, and can create an unbearable amount of pain in a loved one. Your way of dealing with a loved one may no longer be effective, and possibly more destructive as a result.

- People who are in the middle of a crisis often end up leading double lives. One life hides the breakdown, while the other struggles to hold onto reality. This can help you understand why a loved one can easily deceive you during their time of crisis, and also educate you on how unlikely a quick rehabilitation is.

- Making assumptions and placing blame when a loved one starts to breakdown only makes things worse. In order to help a loved one from imploding, you need to adopt an approach of simple curiosity and love, to build understanding and connection.

Three
CHILDHOOD TRAUMA
And What We Know Now

"Childhood trauma is not necessarily a prophecy of doom, because some children are resilient or because later experiences help to restore mental health."
—Richard Bentall

"I think the thumbprint on the throat of many people is childhood trauma that goes un-processed and un-recognized."
—Tom Hooper

Before we jump into the chapter about pain management and how it leads to breakdowns, we wanted to very briefly address a study that was released by Dr. Vince Felitti at Kaiser and Dr. Bob Anda at the CDC on childhood trauma and the adverse affects it has on the physical and emotional healths of adults.[1]

In the mid-90s, they asked 17,500 adults about their history to exposure of what they call "adverse childhood experiences," or ACEs. ACEs are physical, emotional, or sexual abuse, physical or emotional neglect, parental mental illness, substance dependence, incarceration, parental separation or divorce, or domestic violence. Felitti and Anda correlated these results with health outcomes, and this is what they found:

---

1. "Adverse Childhood Experiences (ACEs)." Centers for Disease Control and Prevention, CDC-Kaiser Permanente, 1 Apr. 2016, accessed August 7, 2018, https://www.cdc.gov/violenceprevention/acestudy/index.html.

1. Adults experiencing adverse childhood trauma was common with 67% of the adults surveyed, in which they reported experiencing at least one ACE. 1 in 8 adults had experienced at least four ACEs.

2. The higher your ACE score was the worse your health outcomes were. For a person with an ACE score of four or more, their relative risk of heart disease was two and half times of someone with no ACE score. For depression, it was four and a half times higher, and for possible suicide, it was twelve times higher than someone with no ACE score.

The portion of their study that we find the most relevant to our work is the ramifications of exposure to trauma: a higher risk for depression, addiction, and suicide.

According to Dr. Nadine Burke Harris, a pediatric MD, "Science is now showing that there are real neurological reasons as to why adolescents exposed to high doses of trauma are more likely to engage in high-risk behavior. High doses of trauma not only affect the brain structure in adolescents and function, but also the immune system, developing hormonal systems, and the way the DNA is read and transcribed. When a child experiences trauma, it affects areas like the Nucleus accumbent. It inhibits the prefrontal cortex, which is necessary for impulse control and executive function, a critical area for learning. So there are real neurological reasons why folks exposed to high doses of adversity are more likely to engage in high-risk behavior, and that's important to know."[2]

You should now hopefully realize that some of the problems you and many other caretakers have with their loved ones are reflections of traumatic experiences in a loved one's life. Loved ones may have been have been physically or emotionally altered by their trauma and are therefore left with very little coping skills to deal with what is happening. Hopefully this will give you empathy for the battle they are fighting on a daily basis.

You might have not thought about whether your loved one, who may be struggling with addictions, depression, or suicide, was exposed to some childhood trauma, but consider it now. Is there a possibility that something happened to them during those early years that has affected them in adverse ways? Some caretakers we've worked with have failed to draw a correlation between a drinking problem and their loved one's

2. Harris, Dr. Nadine Burke. "How Childhood Trauma Affects Health across a Lifetime." TED. TEDMED 2014, 2014, San Francisco, https://www.ted.com/talks/nadine_burke_harris_how_childhood_trauma_affects_health_across_a_lifetime

problems because they had been sober in recent years. They then come to realize that the height of their addiction happened while their children were young. Other caretakers never consider that a divorce during their loved ones' earlier years could have had adverse affects later in life because their loved ones seemed to be adjusting fine. Many parents feel overwhelmed in their earlier years as parents and often neglect a loved one in order to take care of themselves. They fail to look at the connection of those experiences with the loss of connection with their loved one—the trauma that might have been experienced early in their lives. It's an important question to ask: it could be a key component to why your loved one is struggling to cope.

To help you further assess your loved one's current crisis and or recent breakdowns, take a moment to reflect on these questions:

1. Is it possible that my loved one is experiencing a breakdown because their brain development was affected by childhood trauma, and they lack the ability to cope like other individuals who didn't experience ACEs?

2. Is it possible that I could have unknowingly been part of the problem they now have?

3. Have I considered other methods of treatment beyond mental healthcare, like proper nutrition or holistic interventions to help if their imbalances are more than what conventional therapy can help with?

4. Is it possible that I have some unresolved trauma that effects the way I deal with my loved ones and how I safeguard myself in painful situations that trigger my trauma? If so, what then?

5. If I too am experiencing a level of depression from ACE, what then?

6. If I was part of the cause of my loved ones ACE, have I taken the time to admit responsibility to my loved one and offer a sincere apology?

At the end of this exercise, you may not find any answers about possible childhood trauma affecting your loved one, which is normal for some. Only two-thirds of the people reading this may have had a relevant experience with ACEs. We hope that this discussion will open a door to understanding what could be happening with your loved one and to help formulate ideas on what to do about it.

If you or a loved one have been affected by childhood trauma, trauma treatment centers are a good place to start looking for help. You can easily find one in most urban areas by searching for Trauma or PTSD Treatment Centers. Proper nutrition also plays a important role in the emotional well being of your loved one. Working with a physician who specializes in trauma and nutrition can be an important piece to helping your loved one, as well as yourself.

It's important that you take some time to find yourself in the equation of trauma if it is relevant to your personal experience and acknowledge it. When things go unchecked or talked about, more resentment and pain can develop not only in yourself, but in those you care for, which could be a factor to the rut you might be facing.

If childhood trauma is left unchecked it can lead to mood disorders, dissociative disorders, PTSD, and anxiety disorders, as well as playing a role in the development of personality disorders. When loved ones are left alone and untreated these disorders can isolate them from you and everyone around them, leaving them vulnerable to addictions, depression, and suicide.

When a loved one is physically struggling to deal with their outside world, their pain becomes more than they can manage, particularly when they are underprepared. At the core of every good breakdown is a underprepared, pain-avoiding addict. On that note, welcome to Chapter 4: Pain, Fantasy & Avoidance.

REFLECTIVE POINTS & CORE PRINCIPLES TO REMEMBER:

- If you suspect that your loved one may be struggling due to ACEs they've experienced, perhaps this is a conversation you want to start having with medical professionals who are trained specifically in working with childhood trauma.

- Start taking a detailed look at your loved ones diet and nutritional climate, and re-calibrate. If you're loved one has been physically altered by their experience they may need a specialized plan to help them with their chemical deficiencies caused by their trauma, which could be adding more fuel to their current break-down as well. Take some time to have them physically looked over as well, as they may have some illnesses that have developed due to their exposure to ACEs.

- If you were affected by ACEs from your childhood, take some time to find someone to help you heal. You can't expect a loved one to heal through trauma if you aren't willing to yourself.

Four

PAIN, FANTASY & AVOIDANCE

"Pain in this life is not avoidable, but the pain
we create avoiding pain is avoidable"
—R.D. Laing

A couple years ago while teaching an adult education course, we met many who were struggling to survive emotionally in their lives, while others in similar situations were emotionally stable. When we realized most of them came from similar environments where poverty, substance abuse, physical abuse, and neglect were rampant, we wondered why there was such a difference in their ability to overcome each of their challenges.

While in private coaching with these students, we started to understand one of the major contributing factors. It came down to the way people managed pain.

When we speak of pain in this chapter, we are referring to anything that causes emotional or physical discomfort. This covers many experiences, including the loss of a loved one, the loss of employment, the loss of dreams or the loss of a relationship; feelings of failure; lack of acceptance or lack of opportunity; lack of a connection to family, home, or friends; physical pain from illness, depression, and anxiety; witnessing or experiencing violence, criticisms, judgments, hurtful sarcasm, starvation, or neglect; or any other type of loss. This also includes feeling emotions like fear and stress. The students who were more successful and well-adjusted in their lives knew how to deal with their pain in a healthy way—most of them had been taught to do so by family members, friends, or other mentors. They didn't run from their problems, and they took responsibility for their actions.

Those who were struggling lacked productive mindsets and strong support systems. They had never been taught how to deal with hardship and struggle. They lacked healthy coping skills when they were deeply hurting. They had loved ones jumping in to rescue them anytime something went wrong. Often, they were sucked into social settings where some form of joy or relief was felt, but at the price of adopting even more destructive behaviors and patterns. This led them to make choices that furthered their problems, like drug addictions, alcoholism, teen pregnancy, suicide, dropping out of school, arrest, theft, and more. These students were following the loudest voice, whether that voice was family members, peers or media culture.

Here's our question for you: **How do you deal with pain in your life, and how does your loved one cope with it now?**

When working with a struggling loved one, it's easy to find yourself fixed on their destructive and hurtful behaviors, whether their behaviors are hurtful to them, to you, or to both of you. However, until you can take responsibility for how you deal with pain in your life and how your loved ones learned to cope based on the tone you set, it will be very challenging to understand why they are doing what they are doing, and easier to cast judgment, creating disconnect.

SLAYING THE DRAGON

Pain and discomfort is real. It is brutal—suffocating at times—and you will always have to face it. We like to refer to pain as *the dragon* in this chapter because, quite frankly. It just is! It's ugly, scary, destructive, and completely debilitating at times. The dragon, if we allow it, can destroy much of the joy we seek. When the dragon is around, we either have to face it and fight, or run and hide. Some students who were dealing with personal breakdowns chose to hide when the dragon became too intense, while others would try distractions, hoping it would go away through violence, substance abuse, or other dangerous behaviors. In both cases, the dragon again became restless and would appear, ready to defeat their happiness because they had failed to deal with it the first time.

If pain from personal issues and events are not dealt with, these emotions can intensify and completely exhaust anybody, sending them searching for relief in the quickest way possible. This is what we want to avoid with any loved one—or ourselves—especially when the relief comes in forms of destructive coping mechanisms and patterns. We also want to avoid the false belief that if one is good enough, wealthy enough, important enough, and perfect enough, they can avoid most difficulties (the proverbial dragon). Life is full of loss and painful moments, and that is quite normal. Unfortunately, many have bought into the belief that if you feel pain, you are doing something wrong. We avoid its necessary place in our personal development. Rabi David Wolpe said it best in his book, *Making Loss Matter*, when he stated:

"Without loss, we live in a steady-state world, a world where progress is stilled. To know this fact is not to welcome it."[3]

If we live in a steady-state world, never progressing, over time this can become more painful than experiencing moments of loss. If we want joy, then we must make room for pain. If loss or pain is necessary for our happiness and if we will experience it many times, then creating a false belief that pain can always be avoided sets you up for greater disappointments and depression when hard times come. If you don't understand this, it is easy to be the loved one who constantly tries to shield family members and friends from feeling pain, setting them up for greater failure in their adult life when they haven't learned to slay their dragon in a healthy way.

Here are some examples of people shielding loved ones from pain:

I got divorced about two years ago, when my little guy was only three. Now that he is almost eight and in baseball, he is so excited to be playing. The only problem is, he's not the best on the team. I feel guilty that his father isn't around to teach him more. I guess I feel guilty myself that we brought a child into the world that is struggling because of our choices. Last week, he came home crying because their team didn't win a tournament trophy. It hurt me beyond belief to see him hurt, especially when I know how hard he tries. He probably could have gotten that trophy if we would have been able to spend more time with him. Then I just got mad and thought it just wasn't right for these little ones to feel like they aren't good enough. They need to feel like winners to perform better. It's our job to build them up, not push them down, so I petitioned to make sure all kids were celebrated with some type of award!

—David

We just bought our daughter a brand new sports car, after she got her license. She is so excited to be driving. I was going to make her work for a car like I had to, but I thought it was such a drag to have to do that

3. Wolpe, David J. *Making Loss Matter: Creating Meaning in Difficult times*. New York: Riverhead Books, 2000.

when I was a teen. I just want her to enjoy growing up; she can worry about that later when she is an adult.

—Brad

My daughter got in trouble at school. I had to go meet with the principal. When he told me that she was disrupting the class with her attitude, I wasn't that surprised. I had heard her teacher wasn't all that great, and she can get bored easily when she doesn't like a class. They wanted me to discipline her or something like that for her behavior, but I thought that was a bit harsh. After all, she's just talkative, and its not her fault that the teacher is terrible.

—Kim

As you can see in these examples, caretakers shield loved ones from the pain that comes from not being the best, the discomfort of working hard for something, and the consequences that come from poor actions. The guardians stomp out the loved one's opportunity to grow and the caretakers shield the loved one (and, as a result, themselves) from discomfort.

In essence, both are struggling to accept and deal with the dragon. This type of overprotection creates a false sense of security for both. While the loved one starts to believe subconsciously that he or she is superior without having to put forth much effort, the caretaker believes that he or she is truly setting their loved one up for success. In actuality, the caretaker is crippling the loved one's ability to succeed. This works until the day someone's child shoots another because they are rejected, a young adult drops out of college because they can't deal with the homework load, or they stop going to work because they believe that they aren't getting paid enough in their first job out of college. They can also begin to think that life is too depressing and hard and try to commit suicide; that working for a living is awful so they sell their self-worth and talents to someone who will buy their love; that using a gun to get what they want seems like the best rational course; that drugs are more fun than anything else in life; or that sitting on the sofa, playing video games and hanging with friends while mooching off of guardians is acceptable.

Since these young ones have been robbed of falling and recovering when the hard times were easier and less trivial, they could not learn the proper way to deal with failure. Since pain, loss, and challenges will always be part of their lives, they are left severely underprepared when greater challenges hit them. They become easily overwhelmed by the dragon, and they plead for their enabler guardian to rescue them. The enablers see what they have done wrong, but the pain of watching their young ones hurt because of their adversity weighs them down. They jump in to shield their loved ones yet again, sending the dragon away for a season, but perpetuating the cycle.

There is a caveat to this, however. We want to strongly impress that we are *not* suggesting that you should *not* buy your loved one a new car if you want to. We want you to walk away with an understanding that if your intentions are to shield a loved one from experiencing something that could be uncomfortable, you are *not* helping them in the end. If you are the type of parent that knows when to give a proper reward and a car is the reward, then trust your instinct. Simply be careful that you aren't overprotecting them from everything that could cause them pain.

GETTING INTO THE PAIN GAME

You cannot help your loved one deal with pain if you aren't aware of how you might be shielding yourself from pain. Whatever you do, your loved one will learn, but often will learn and cope slightly differently. Often, we work with guardians who fail to understand the correlation between their coping mechanisms and their loved ones' destructive patterns. It is easier and much less painful to point the finger at the obvious offender than to notice your own. Over time, most people have created a way of dealing with pain that was learned somewhere and from someone. This is usually someone who has had a big part or influence in your life: a parent, family member, mentor, or friend. Here's the big question though: Did your mentors deal with pain in a healthy manner? Let's take a look at some examples of adults using destructive coping mechanisms to deal with their pain:

> A couple of years ago I was in a terrible place. Everything had bottomed out. I felt like I was reaching for anything that would take away the dull ache I felt every day I got out of bed. It felt excruciating. In the past, if I felt bad, I would just go buy myself some clothes. That always made me feel good about myself, but over time I couldn't really afford what I was buying. That depressed me even more, so then I bought more. Then I couldn't pay my bills. It was stressful to have the debt collectors calling me at work. I tried to avoid their calls, I tried to avoid everything. The littlest things became so overwhelming.
>
> —Kelsey

> I grew up in a home where rewards were always linked to food. I love food! If I have a bad day, I can always have a great meal, and when

it comes to sugar, I am a monster. I can eat dessert like it's my last day alive. I know I'm a bit overweight, but I've tried to diet and it's too hard. When I'm on a diet and those hard days hit, I'm terrible to deal with.

—Jane

I can't throw anything away. I feel a little out of control when I go to garage sales. It feels so good to come home with all these amazing things people want to throw away. If the world goes to the dogs, I'm gonna have everything I need. People call me a hoarder. I have so much stuff we are literally sitting on it. But I can't get rid of it.

—David

I love video games! I can't get enough of them. I think it all started when I was eight and I finally got a Nintendo. I was so excited. I started out your basic gamer and then became completely consumed. As soon as homework was done, I was in the game. It felt good to be good at something, and I didn't have to deal with not having very many friends. It was hard for me to make friends, but in the game I never really felt alone. Now as an adult, I go to work and play video games with people all over the world. I'm in my thirties and don't see a family in the future at any point. I'm happy with the way things are in my life.

—Jacob

I'm always that person who is in a relationship. I can't go very long without the connection. I also get bored really easily. I jump from relationship to relationship when I see that it's not giving me what I want. I actually can't remember the last time I didn't have a girlfriend.

—Allen

I love to take care of people. It's in my blood and it motivates me to get up and do what I do everyday. If I don't have someone to take care of, I typically find ways to insert myself into people's lives. I always go with the intention of doing good, but I think I end up enabling them in the end because I don't know when to step back and not help. I like knowing that they have something to owe me even though I would probably never ask for it.

—Stacy

I know I've got my own problems to deal with, but I'm more concerned about my friends around me. I will stay awake at night thinking and worrying about them to the point that it consumes my life. They often tell me to focus on my problems and stop worrying about them. Don't they want a friend that cares? It seems that my caring is getting me nowhere now because they seem to be pushing me away. I can't help myself. I just feel like I need to solve problems to feel like I'm worth something.

—Kimberly

I remember having a beer with my uncle when I wasn't even a teenager. That's when I got my first taste of drinking. In high school, I totally partied hard. I won't even go into details, but it was crazy. In college, it just got better because it was legal. I really should stop because I'm in my fifties partying like I'm in college. I finally got my first DUI, and it scared me to death! I don't really feel like I have a drinking problem. Drinking just helps me calm down after my day. Otherwise I'm wound up too tight."

—Bradley

Some people might say I am the town gossip. I have to admit I love the drama … tell me a juicy story and I am in. It makes life more interesting to hear everybody else's drama. I never really intend to tell their stories but sometimes I can't help myself. Okay, I admit it. All the time I can't help myself. I love having something interesting to say."

—Beth

I am the queen of avoiding. I avoid everything and anything that feels uncomfortable … if someone is mad at me, I disappear. If life gets too hard, I avoid anyone I made commitments to. If I need to have a difficult conversation, I will avoid it and act like things never happened.

—Jennifer

I find myself constantly having an opinion about what people are doing. I have to pick it apart, and make a judgment. I can't help myself that so many around me are messed up. All I can do is make sure I don't become so messed up, and follow their path. I only have a few close friends, and even those I hold closest to me I think are messed up at times."

—Marie

I was sexually assaulted by one of our family friends. He told my parents he was going to take me on a ride around the block in his new car. At eight years old, who wouldn't be excited to ride in a fancy car? When he pulled off the side of the road, my life would change forever. The shame and secrecy I felt after he assaulted and threatened me led me to live a life in the sex industry as a pornographic film star. I attended lavish parties where men could not get enough of my attention. I started to become addicted to attracting a man, seducing him, and then dropping him as if he meant nothing to me. It was the only thing that made me feel momentarily happy and satisfied. During a coaching session, I came to realize that not only was I doing this to ultimately protect myself from being hurt again—giving me the upper hand I never had when I was eight—but I was encouraging the behaviors of those who committed these types of sexual crimes. Most convicts admitted to pornography being the start of their addiction and downfall.

—Natalie

As you read some of these stories of people we have met or worked with, can you identify the ways they distract themselves from pain? Can you identify some tools you might use to self-soothe and asked yourself whether they are healthy or destructive? Are you a spender, an eater, a hoarder, a drinker, a sex addict, an enabler, a drama maker, a gossiper, a phone addict, an avoider, or a critic? When you feel pain, loss, or discomfort in your life, how do you deal with it? How is this behavior keeping you from moving forward? How have these behaviors taught your loved ones to cope with their own problems? How could your behaviors be related to some of their current breakdowns or struggles?

OUR STRUGGLES

Personally, this chapter took awhile to write because before we could write it, we had to come to terms with the ways we would self-medicate through our own personal pain. We wanted to have the confidence to help you as well. When we took a deeper look at ourselves, we uncovered avoidance patterns, fantasy addictions, overeating and overspending habits.

I remember coming home from a hard day and all I wanted to do was eat and eat. I would over do it at dinner, and then I would over do it on dessert. There was always a point when what seemed to be uncomfortable faded away, but then there was also a point that I also felt guilty for eating like I did, knowing that I had put on a few pounds, despite promising myself I would turn things around.

—Hollie

There's a funny thing I do. I hate it. I've always loved cars and growing up they were a big part of my life. I remember my room was full of car magazines and friends who shared the passion. We would talk endlessly about them. Harmless, if not a bit of a time waster. We had a lot of good times on road trips and to this day I always have a fun car to take a road trip in, something unique, something that becomes part of the experience. I have to admit that my love has turned into self-medication now, a way to distract me from real work, whether that is my job or personal work. It's pretty innocuous.

I will browse car websites looking for the latest models and then I go to the manufacturers' websites and spend way too much building and pricing out a dream car that I may be fantasizing about at that particular moment. An hour will go by fast as I live in the fantasy of my head and dream about where I would go or the person I would be if I had this or that car or truck. It is a sure sign to me today that I am avoiding something in my life, so I've made changes and I'm getting better at it, but man is it a fun and easy escape!

—Josh

Currently, I've been sick for over a year now. There were days when I would wake up and wonder if I could get through the day because my mind had become my worst enemy and my body was shutting down. I would be overwhelmed with violent flashes, and would sometimes feel the frantic unraveling of my brain that should push someone to sit in a corner and nervously pull their hair out. These were things people were admitted to psychiatric hospitals for and I was aware of it. I knew the illness had caused an inflammation in my brain, which was causing daily panic attacks. I quickly empathized for those who develop mental illnesses, and how challenging it was for them to exist in their world. It was a world like no other, wracked with daily pain and discomfort.

I had tasted good health most of my life, but now I not only felt like I was losing my mind, but that my organs were exploding and I felt like I was gasping for air—I felt like I was breathing through a tiny straw most of the day. This was also happening around the time I was doing a lot of research about pain, loss, and fantasy addictions. Ironically, I found myself in one of the biggest fights of my life. I experienced the loss of vitality and health and huge financial burdens from the medical bills trying fight my illness. I could no longer self medicate through purchasing. I couldn't go out to eat a wonderful meal or enjoy the junk food I'd previously escaped to because my diet had been restricted so much to try and reduce the inflammation in my body.

On top of that, I had no appetite for food. I couldn't listen to music because it was so disruptive that I would often go into a panic attack. I couldn't talk on the phone because my lungs had been affected by my illness, and the daily stresses of people's lives would cause me to feel incredible anxiety. Watching television was limited to a few cooking shows as anything that would stimulate my adrenal glands would bring on panic. I found little to no joy in my life.

This was a "stake in the ground" moment for me. I remember finding myself lost in fantasy, one of my go-to avoidance techniques, which was a relief, but which then also created feelings of anguish and sadness, because I did not have the resources necessary I felt to fight my illness. Before I had become surprisingly ill, I had just finished Rabi David Wolpe's book[1]. It had changed my life in understanding the necessity of pain. I remember having a conversation with myself after learning what I had from the book: "This is loss. It's okay. Don't try to avoid it. In the end, loss will make you happier than if you were to feel no loss at all." I wanted it to end … sure I did. Everyone wants his or her devastation to go away as quickly as possible. But, it wasn't going away, and I had a choice. Either create as much joy within my loss, or be overwhelmed with my loss. I didn't feel like I had the power to take my illness away, and the power to create seemed to be the only thing I could control.

So, I approached myself gently, felt sadness and fear when it came, cried about it here and there, prayed it would go away, and then went on with living, appreciating anything that would offer relief: a call from a brother who could distract my mind with his funny stories, a visit from a friend who needed someone to talk to, the day that I would wake up feeling okay for a couple of hours. Especially the salty chicken broth that would take away my nausea for some time. This is how I went about slaying my own dragon.

I'm still sick to this day, though the severe effects of the illness I have described have tapered off a bit. Every day is still a constant battle of dealing with not feeling well and my physical limitations, as I still feel the pain of not finding my way back to health. However, now it's no longer an overwhelming part of my life. This is what I think we are trying to work for here, to not allow pain—and how we cope with pain—to rule and win.

—Hollie

We then realized that we didn't really know what it meant to look at pain without trying to avoid it. In essence, we didn't know how to feel okay with not feeling okay. When we were able to recognize our destructive coping patterns—when those painful moments came up again—we would notice our instinctive nature to self-medicate and stopped ourselves. This was a critical moment of knowing for us, to make sure we recognized the pattern and could remember where we had been so we could move forward.

After this process of discovery, we then worked on changing our old thoughts and beliefs to new ones, and then changed our bad behavior to something better, like picking up the phone and calling a friend, allowing ourselves to be comfortable with crying for a bit, or writing about our pain until we felt better. If we liked eating to escape, we wouldn't allow ourselves to go to the fridge. Instead, we would have a conversation with ourselves about what was going on internally, acknowledging that whatever we were going through really hurt. We would then comfort ourselves by saying, "This is pain. This is normal, and it is necessary. It will pass eventually." We could then come up with a healthier alternative to coping. It was a slow process at first because sometimes we would give into our old ways. We hadn't built up enough trust in ourselves that what we were doing would actually work. It's much easier to believe the way you are coping with life is the best way for you, even if it's unhealthy and is creating more problems in your life. But, that is the illusion and the fantasy that we had to realize. In essence, we had to understand that we were never really growing by self-medicating. We weren't standing up to the dragon. We were merely delaying and multiplying our problems while building an illusion that we were okay.

This process was difficult. It was hard to feel this constant pain, with no relief at first. Sometimes the pain would last a day, but sometimes it would last for months. We had to learn to be okay with that. We had to learn to make the presence of pain just as natural and as normal as the presence of happiness.

We know that considering pain as a constant companion may seem un-comfortable to talk about or consider. Consider it for a moment though. Do you want happiness? If knowing happiness means you must know pain, are you robbing yourself of greater happiness by avoiding the depth of the pain you feel through unhealthy distractions? Are you robbing your loved ones by rescuing them too soon from their pain?

When we stopped focusing on avoiding and accepted its natural and necessary place in our lives, we weren't so shocked and overwhelmed when it arrived. We weren't as devastated with its presence because we knew it had to exist in order to feel happiness and joy. We found its emotional effects and weight far less painful over time through acceptance, and we were able to make better choices to help understand it, deal with it, and learn from it. With this newfound knowledge came the recognition that we needed to create good moments in our lives—moments of relief—because without those good moments, pain would steal our hope and resiliency.

When running a marathon, runners are unable to complete a marathon without the rest stops for water or food. We too could not make it through the painful moments in our lives without creating moments to refill our resiliency tanks. In learning this process, we had to teach ourselves to enjoy things on a more elementary level. For example, if a friend reached out to us and we had a great conversation, we celebrated that as if we had gotten a new car. If we found a manager special at the grocery store, we treated it as if we'd won the lottery. We wanted the subconscious mind to start believing our life was not overwhelmed with pain, but that it was instead good and full. By changing our way of thinking, we were able to program the mind to elevate our mood and spirits. This is the power of the subconscious mind. If we believe something is true at a subconscious level, our mind works to create an environment to match our beliefs.

Lou Tice and Dr. Joe Pace said, "Once you establish what's normal for you, once you establish how you are, the process in the creative subconscious makes sure you stay pretty close to behaving like yourself. If you do worse, you correct up. But if you do better than you think you are, you correct down. You correct for the mistake inside yourself. You check and balance your actions, your behavior, your life, not at your potential level, but a your belief level. Now how did you get your beliefs? What do you believe to be true? If you don't change your belief, which is changing your mind to a higher level that you expect, you will always self-regulate at that level. You are a self-regulating mechanism."[4]

It was through this balancing act of positive versus negative that the pain became more tolerable. We became victorious and could slay the dragon. We started to notice friends who were amazed at the level of resiliency we had created. Many times they would ask us, "How are you not so overwhelmed with your life right now, with all the challenges you have been facing?"

It was then we were able to respond, "We get the pain game now, and we are better prepared than ever to deal with it!"

FANTASY ADDICTS

One of the biggest things we uncovered in ourselves and in those we worked with was the use of fantasy in our lives to avoid pain. We aren't

---

4. Tice, Louis E., and Joe Pace. Thought Patterns for a Successful Career. Seattle, WA: Pacific Institute, 2006.

suggesting that fantasy in itself is entirely bad, but it can be if it is misused. From a small age, we are given a healthy dose of fantasy. This is what makes childhood such a beautiful thing: trips to Disneyland, magical holidays and birthday parties, larger-than-life movies, and vacations. To live through a child is a wonderful thing as well, to sense their excitement and joy. Unfortunately, the love for fantasy and the high it produces—if not combined with realistic discussions and experiences about how life is not always a fairy tale—can create a powerful disconnect in people, so much so that they can create more problems by hiding behind the wall of fantasy. British actress Emily Blunt called this issue out when parents were concerned about the remake of the movie, *Into the Woods*. Parents expressed many less than happy reviews that the theme of the movie was too laden with difficulty, and they didn't want to expose their children to such hardship. Blunt responded by saying:

"Children are coddled too much by sanitized modern stories and fairy tales. Chris Pine [who plays the prince] was telling me that most schools in America only do the first act of the play, where everything is happy ever after. And it's just sad that we're choosing to coddle our children that way, because no one's more perceptive than a child. In older Disney films, Bambi loses his mother, Dumbo is wrenched away from his mother, who is chained up and tormented and bullied. It used to be darker and more challenging. Nobody goes through life unscathed. If you want to fairy tale the shit out of everything, you're doing everyone a disservice."[5]

We believe she is spot on. What happens to us when fantasy is too much of our emotional diet? Often, people lean into the world of fantasy because of its pleasure. In order to cope with pain, we lean in too much, in a way that distracts us from dealing with issues that need to be resolved. We'd like to share a couple stories with you to show you how fantasy can be misused to cope with pain:

NOT A FAIRY TALE ENDING

Disney movies' love stories are a beautiful tragedy in a girl's life. At a young age, we get to think about how some day our prince will come. We dream up love stories where we are the most beautiful, desired, and sought-after girl on the planet. I would get lost in the stories of older women telling me when they found that special someone and how it should

5. Farmer, Ben. "Children Too Coddled by Modern Stories, Says Emily Blunt." The Telegraph. January 03, 2015. Accessed January 12, 2019. https://www.telegraph.co.uk/news/celebritynews/11323215/Children-too-coddled-by-modern-stories-says-Emily-Blunt.html.

and would feel, and how happy it made them. I remember eagerly waiting until I was old enough to date, and imagining how fun it would be to have all these guys asking me out.

But then that day came and nobody called. I started to see other friends have dates and boyfriends, but I did not. It was incredibly painful. I started to feel that maybe I wasn't attractive or valuable enough. Occasionally I would talk to my mom about it, but she had lots of dates in her day, so it didn't make sense that I wouldn't be dating, which added to my discomfort and rejection level.

During that time in my life, I also didn't feel terribly connected to my own father. That was painful as well because it felt like rejections from men were all around me. In order to comfort myself, I would find myself fantasizing about who I would meet and how they would fly me all around the world, and make me feel like I am the one they couldn't live without. This fantasy became a natural part of my emotional diet.

When I entered my late twenties, I found myself dating the way I had always imagined, and finally felt like I was being valued the way I had always dreamed. The problem began when I realized my years of fantasizing was such a necessary and normal part of my thought process. It made me excited and hopeful, but it also created a hunger in me for the fantasy to be fulfilled. In other words, if I met someone that would excite me the way the fantasy did, I was head over heels. But, I was only head over heels until the next person came along and distracted me from a relationship that was shifting and changing, as most relationships do over time. If I was in a relationship with someone I said I loved, and someone else wanted to ask me out, I would quickly find a way to discredit the relationship I was in. I wanted to jump ship and be pursued by another. I couldn't say no because of my need to be wanted, desired, and pursued. I could not put aside my fantasy—my deep hunger for constant love and attention would not work in a long-term and healthy relationship.

This created a different problem. I found myself choosing people I knew I would never make a life-long commitment to so that I could continue to feed my addiction to the fantasy that multiple people would want and need me in their lives.

In trying to cope with my pain over time, I had become my worst enemy, never allowing myself to move forward or backward in my relationships because I was so dependent on the perfect picture I spent years creating. I always wanted the crazy fun energy of being with a new love and being intensely wanted. Without the exciting rush of being desired, I felt like life and my relationships were boring and lack luster, which was painful. I needed someone new to date, to spark my excitement and begin the cycle all over again.

I started to feel resentful that my true emotional needs and what I wanted to do were polar opposites. Either I gave up one thing that gave me consistent pleasure to jump into something that gave me no guarantee for happiness, or I stayed doing what I was doing, convincing myself I was getting enough of what I needed. The entire time I wrestled with my subconscious; it knew the truth. If I didn't change something, I could be living out the same cycle year after year—possibly forfeiting the right relationship because I needed that validation.

THE BUSINESS PLAN

I fantasize about amazing business ideas and workouts. I talk about it with everyone. I get people engaged and then I completely bail out. Most of the time, it distracts me from the tough things that aren't going right at the moment, and I find myself daydreaming, plotting out things on a poster board, wasting time hopping from thing to thing, and letting people down in the process. They believe I'm 100% committed to my cause, but I never quite lean into the stuff that needs to be dealt with.

After untangling our own issues with fantasy, we started to recognize fantasy addictions in many of our clients, friends, and family members. Some were lost in the fantasy of becoming famous, so much so that their fantasy addiction overtook their ability to have a stable job to support themselves. They were consumed by their fantasy of stardom, but they failed to have enough talent or drive to get them where they hoped to go.

Some were carried away in the gaming world, a fantasy rush that consumed their lives, giving a false sense of connection to other players around the world. This fantasy kept them from more important things at home and in their relationships. They would often put the game before other people.

Some people were in committed relationships, but would destroy everything they had through infidelity because they believed they should always be the head-over-heels-in-love couple. If they didn't feel that way, or if things became hard, they felt that wasn't normal and it was time to get out. They would become addicted to the first phases of a new relationship, and once that fizzled out, they would jump ship.

We would hear from teens who believed they were going to get scholarships playing ball. They would brag and boast about it, but would never put in the practice necessary to make that happen—the fantasy was much easier than the work. They would get wrapped up in games and stats, knowing everything about the teams they wanted to play for, but never giving enough effort to make it happen.

Some would get stuck in the fantasy that if they were good enough, their abusive family members would give them the emotional support they desperately needed. They would develop a perfectionist complex with an intense fear of disapproval or abandonment from people they felt connected to. Afraid of rejection, they would smother any prospective friend and drive them away, perpetuating their subconscious belief that they weren't good enough to be appreciated and loved by others.

Pornography for many is also deeply routed in the world of fantasy. It allows its victims to participate in a world where unrealistic sexual relationships and role-playing is performed to arouse its consumers. Many who start with light porn slowly move into more aggressive porn as their addictions for sexual fantasy are never satiated; meanwhile, pornography instills a dangerous belief about how sexual relationships should play out with significant others. The addict becomes so involved that they no longer relate to their partners—their need for deep sexual fantasy has them turning to porn for their pay offs, destroying their intimate relationships in the process.

At its core, fantasy addiction creates a world that is unattainable and unhealthy while luring the addict into believing that all is well. It's a clever way of offsetting pain and discomfort. Many don't even know they are developing behaviors that set them back until they have set patterns and are dependent on their addiction. Like we expressed in the first story about relationship fantasy addictions, letting go is terrifying because it does not guarantee a payout, where the alternative—even though attached to results that are harmful or negative—offers some type of relief or payout.

HOW DO I KNOW IF I, OR A LOVED ONE, HAVE A FANTASY ADDICTION?

Fantasy addictions are deeply routed in thought. It starts to become a problem when we want to duplicate our thoughts and our behaviors because we crave going back to that train of thought or to the behavior linked to our fantasy. When the behaviors we participate in are ultimately destructive in nature or create negative results, leading us to avoid things in our lives, this is a good indication that a fantasy addiction has set in. In our first example, daydreaming about the perfect relationship seemed pretty harmless. Over time, however, the repetitive and destructive thoughts created an unrealistic picture of perfection keeping the relationship further than what was truly wanted.

We are all at risk of becoming fantasy addicts, though younger minds tend to be more susceptible, especially if they are living in an affluent home and community where they have access to everything they could want. Their inexperience with hardship and loss paired with their access to movies, technology, money, violence, food, pornography, and social media creates a perfect breeding ground for destructive fantasies that keep them from dealing with the dragon.

Boys can get lost in the fantasy world of gaming, especially if their outside world makes them feel powerless and angry. This is why so many that we have seen bullied at school become hyper-focused on gaming at home. It's a relief getting lost in the fantasy of the game because they are the victors, and they have the ultimate control of their lives within the game. They can forget their pain, their loss, and their rejection, when otherwise they don't feel like they can.

Girls can get sucked into the fantasy of being beautiful and wanted by everyone. Let's face it: the message rings loud and clear all around that if you are pretty enough, you are valued. When you don't feel like you are worth something, it is painful. We see very few girls that manage their pain by doing something nice for someone else. Much of their thought is tied up into themselves instead. Selfie after selfie, hours of primping, maneuvering around friends and popular circles to create value, and privately obsessing over weight are just distractions from the painful beliefs they are trying to manage.

So, how do you know if you or your loved ones are dealing with fantasy addictions? Start by asking yourself these questions: How do you or your loved ones use thought and belief to abandon pain? How do those thoughts and beliefs cause you to behave in your life, and does it send you in a direction where you avoid the dragon? Now, think of your struggling loved ones. Do they talk or act in a way where their need to be validated or to feel better about themselves has them locked in a thought pattern far from true reality? Does this thought pattern propagate so much that they are creating and living in a fantasy far from a life that is healthy or currently exists?

I remember working with a teen singer who believed that she was going to be a big pop star, but she couldn't sing. She knew every song, every move, every article done on her pop icon. She would spend hours doing research rather than studying, and she was failing in classes at school. She was so addicted to the thoughts about her stardom that she couldn't seem to regulate her everyday life. With little self-esteem, she imploded when she started to get sucked into the wrong crowd at school.

If you are able to recognize a consistent pattern of thoughts and behaviors linked to unrealistic or unhealthy expectations of life or life outcomes—

specifically those that are holding you back from a healthy reality—you are probably dealing with some sort of fantasy addiction.

Fantasy addictions don't always produce wonderful positive thoughts about how the world should be or could be. Others can be addicted to creating false fantasies about the wonderful life others may have compared to themselves. This grass-is-greener mentality can make people feel like a victim. If these types of people grew up in a painful environment, they may have a hard time creating anything more than pain and will continue to self medicate in other ways, creating a roller coaster of emotions.

Addictions to cell phones is just another form of fantastical distraction. When life feels lackluster or boring, it's easy to engage in the fantasy we create around others' lives. Our mind allows fantasy to take over when we allow ourselves to obsess over how amazing and happy other people are on social media. Though seemingly harmless, this can cause more discomfort in those who try to compare themselves to others.

Fantasy doesn't always create fuzzy, feel-good feelings. Negative thoughts can be just as addicting if a person identifies with being a victim. These are victims who turn their thoughts into a self-pitying mentality. This may not make sense because we typically think that fantasy is used to avoid pain. Why would one want to use fantasy to create more pain? However, it makes sense if we understand that some people have only known pain in their lives, for example, from abuse or abandonment. Though they hate the life they are in, they don't know any other way of living. When too much joy comes along, it feels unsettling and unnatural, and it competes with their belief of what normal is. This is similar to those who mostly feel joy and become uncomfortable with pain. In both instances, these people will do all they can to regulate back to their normal. This happens quite often by creating fantasies about how life is not fair and never has been, how people are out to get them, and how unworthy they are. They can play this lie over and over until it eventually sabotages their life.

HOW DO YOU HELP YOURSELF AND OTHERS OUT OF FANTASY ADDICTION?

Simply put, you've got to recognize what triggers you or a loved one to escape into fantasy and what action you can take as a result of those destructive thoughts. This is easier said than done—we know this firsthand. It will feel like you are learning to ride a bike for the first time: unstable, clumsy, scary, and sometimes painful. On top of that, there's no guarantee of a pay out for you.

We have a client who inspires us. But, his process has been much of what we are sharing with you now. Drugs were his way of coping with pain from family problems in addition to using fantasy as a way of escaping. We would chat often and it seemed his first fantasy was that somehow other people would make things happen for him. He was filled with great entrepreneurial ideas but they hinged on someone making it work. This crossed over to how he dealt with his own problems; they were never his own, always another's fault. After returning home from treatment, he really began to see how he'd invent a path for himself but wasn't ever willing to do anything about it. We finally got the chance to discuss this with him so he could understand. He was cooking up a retail clothing business and we asked him, "What are you going to do right now to make it happen?" He responded with silence. Lots of silence.

He couldn't move from fantasy to reality. He was struggling to proceed because the work could be hard or result in failure. He started to realize he had let a lot of life slip by because he thought others should do it for him.

Then we asked again, "What can you do right now and what can we do right now to help make this happen?"

Adding some support finally changed the equation for him. He responded, "I could hop in the car and see what designs are big right now, make a list of colors, and then figure out what my next move will be." Finally, he had new momentum and changed his old pattern. We told him that no one expected him to do it alone, and none of us should feel that way. We told him that he should expect to hold the reins of the business, but include others in supporting roles.

Today, he has a store and is learning a lot about himself and what it takes to go from fantasy to reality. The fantasy still creeps in, but that moment of momentum created a tether to reality. When he hopped in his car and made a plan, he was able to do something with his idea. He wasn't floating in fantasy land anymore because he'd tied himself down. He can still look up and dream, but his feet are planted solidly on the path he is clearing.

If you find your loved one lost in fantasy, you can help tether them to the ground and redirect their thoughts. If they have developed negative behaviors, like playing hours of video games, start to think of ways you can redirect their energy to something that can provide relief in a healthier and more productive way. Talk about fantasy and addiction and teach them what addiction to fantasy looks like and why it can be destructive. Most people aren't even aware that their behaviors can multiply over time and give them less of what they truly want in life. They need the help of a respected and loved advisor.

HOW DO I DECIPHER BETWEEN A DREAM AND A FANTASY?

Let's say your loved one has a dream of being a star basketball player. You are doubtful they can accomplish that dream due to their physical limitations (i.e., height, speed, or talent) and you don't want to be a dream crusher. You also want to make sure they aren't using fantasy to deal with something else. How do you know when to step in?

You may have seen an inspirational movie, *Rudy*, where a small-in-stature boy with limited financial support and dyslexia has dreams of playing for Notre Dame. His family laughs at him, thinking he could never accomplish his dream. He ends up not only earning the necessary grades to attend Notre Dame, but earns a spot on the football team as a walk on, a difficult thing to do for someone his size.[6]

Nobody wants to be a guardian who drives a loved one away just because they didn't have the same vision and feared their child would get swept away into fantasy. How do you know when to step in? We tend to use this formula. If you or a loved one can't get past this two-step process: of thinking about the dream and then researching, practicing, or putting in real effort towards that dream, then your loved one may be stuck in fantasy land. If there is no real action involved, but they continue to put a lot of time and effort into thinking about the dream without accomplishing anything, you've got a problem. It's time to step in.

For example, if they are always talking about being in a committed relationship, but they keep jumping from person to person, there's a problem. If a young loved one keeps talking about getting a scholarship for baseball, but won't go and practice, there's a problem. If a loved one says they really want to go to college, do all the research on where they want to go, have you take them on tours of the college, but never study enough to make decent grades, there's a problem. Basically, if your loved one has a dream and is working to accomplish it, let them be. This could end up leading them to a great place, perfect for them. They will either accomplish what they have set out to do or at the very least will have been taught an invaluable lesson if they come up short of the goal.

HOLLIE'S STORY

I dreamed of being a professional dancer. It was all I wanted. I worked so hard, putting in hours of practice, but I never saw that dream come

---

6. Rudy. Directed by David Anspaugh.

to fruition. I didn't have the right body shape or feet for the job, just the right heart. My parents never discouraged my dreams. When I started to see that I wasn't getting where I wanted to go, and the challenges I was facing, I started to ask myself about what else I might contribute to the world. With the fear I'd end up failing just as bad, I turned my energy to music. The years of training and hard work primed me for this adventure. I knew how to sweat, how to fail, and how to succeed. I had been doing it long before music came into my life. The years at the ballet barre taught me poise, the performances on stage gave me nerve, and the hours of work with the promise of very little taught me perseverance.

Let them fail, and let them pick themselves up. Don't be too anxious in that process. This process is what will help them learn and become stronger. Many successful dreamers needed this drive in order to accomplish what they really wanted.

AVOIDANCE

Avoidance is a behavior that typically robs you or someone else of something, like a relationship, an experience, or an opportunity. It is a delayer of things that will ultimately be. The only advantage of avoidance is that it buys time, but often at the expense of yourself or others. As parents or caretakers of loved ones, we know you want joy in the lives of those you care for and love. Unfortunately, that desire can also create problems when you feel it is your role to protect your loved ones by teaching them—through either word, action, or inaction—that avoiding things in life is an appropriate way of dealing with pain.

We can do this by never allowing our loved ones to experience failure or difficulty. There are many ways of doing this, but it can happen by simply creating opportunities for your loved ones to avoid those experiences or by neglecting emotional needs. For example, caretakers sometimes need to have difficult discussions with their loved ones. By avoiding those conversations, you are not only neglecting their emotional needs, but teaching them that avoiding hard things is okay. In essence, these caretakers sweep problems or issues under the rug and carry on with life as if nothing is wrong.

We talked about this earlier in the chapter by pointing out that our addictions and negative behaviors are linked to the avoidance of pain. It's important to look at whether you are an avoider, especially if you want to help your loved one appropriately. Do you avoid hard conversations with friends or co-workers? Do you avoid a significant other if you are hurt? Do you avoid responsibility at home, work, or church when you've committed to doing something, especially if it's difficult or inconvenient? If so, what do you think your loved one is learning when they watch you avoid? Here are a few of the avoidance tools people tend to use:

- Rescuing and enabling

- Excusing behaviors so you don't have to deal with them

- Expressions of being "burnt out," or "done" to allow you to walk away

- Being passive aggressive

- Paving the way by doing everything for them, and not allowing them to experience on their own

- Leaving things for others to fix (therapists, coaches, other family)

- Believing he/she will figure it out

- Never really addressing the real issues or frustrations you have because it might cause more problems with your loved one.

Though we aren't going to address each one on this list, we would like to focus on the *paving the way* tool for a moment, as this seems to be a huge problem for some of our clients. It starts with a desire to create a beautiful life for a loved one, but for many, it ends up creating a loved one that is too coddled and protected, completely unequipped to deal with reality. However, is there possibly something else at play?

We believe that those who are fixated on protecting loved ones have a very difficult time dealing with pain, especially when it is the pain of a loved one. It is excruciating for them to sit with a loved one in pain and *not* rescue them. They avoid this by padding their loved ones wherever they can. There is a huge problem with this mindset. Many will see the negative results of their actions when they realize their loved one is completely un-equipped to navigate pain later in life.

There are two movies that come to mind: *Everything, Everything* and *Bubble Boy*. The films' premises are the *paving the way* mindset. The teens are living in a protective-bubble life because their caretakers are so afraid they will hurt or harm themselves by going outside and living life. The bubble is their massive plan of attack, the ultimate avoider. Eventually, the teens break loose and go absolutely crazy doing all the things they were told they couldn't do.[7] These guardians became the ultimate lesson thieves. A lesson thief is someone who, with great intentions, tries to create a perfect, loving environment at all times, like we talked about previously. They typically don't realize that this perfection is impossible to accomplish.

The lesson thief hasn't realized that pain caused by natural consequences or situations (for example, a friend who betrays them, losing a game, becoming sick, losing a loved one, having to move, losing friends, and living in poverty) cannot be 100% controlled. They go about padding and protecting their loved one, avoiding anything that could potentially scar their child for life, never allowing their loved one to hurt, recover on their own, and learn. Lesson thieves are the ultimate avoiders.

How do you think your loved one will feel when they realize they have been robbed of opportunities to grow because you have either taught them to avoid their pain through unhealthy coping techniques or have made it possible to avoid the pain of consequence or hardship? A loving caretaker allows one to go through hard times because they understand that pain is necessary for growth. A caretaker understands that if he steps in too often to try and remove his loved one's discomfort, he is interfering with life lessons that his loved one needs to learn and grow. He understands that his loved one truly needs support, confidence, and the proper tools necessary to overcome their adversity.

In other words, let them fail!

Stop linking your self worth to the status of their success and perfection. Let them fail while still holding an invisible safety net. You don't want young ones to know you are going to save them, otherwise they will look to you to help them all the time. They will never learn to grow from their adversity. Be there to console them, and only help when measures call for you to help, but do it sparingly.

> I was bullied all through elementary school. It was so painful to know that I was not liked by several of the girls who would laugh and taunt me. I remember coming home and telling my mom a little bit about it. She never marched over to the school and ordered that something be done about it, but she was there. She would give me a hug and say, "I know it's hard honey, but not everybody will like you in life. At least you know it's safe here and we love you. Make it through the day and come home to love." This didn't take my problems away. I still remember falling into fantasy and daydreaming of how I would bug their rooms so I had

---

7. Bubble Boy. Directed by Blair Hayes. Everything, Everything. Directed by Stella Meghie.

solid evidence that all their giggles were matched with hurtful comments about me. This was my way of coping and feeling in control. The painful memory still exists today, but what I learned was priceless. I learned to not let their actions define me, and I learned to be kind to others because I knew how it felt to be treated poorly.

Had I not gone through those hard times, possibly experiencing a guardian that jumped in to rescue me instead, what would I have learned? That you cower when someone bullies you?

No, indeed.

Day after day, I learned to survive. I learned how to lay a foundation of resiliency. It wasn't easy. It was painful, but I did it. Years later, I remember looking back and thinking, "If I could make it through everything I've been through, then I can get through this." I had the confidence because I was allowed to feel and experience pain with the proper support from loved ones, which made me even more successful in the end.

—Jessica

Today, the topic of bullying has been brought to the front of many school agendas because of social media, school violence, and suicide. How do we solve the problem of bullying though? Is it through anti-bullying campaigns? Sure, those are helpful. However, until you get to the heart of the matter, those campaigns are just a band aid to the problem. The heart of the matter is that our loved ones are bombarded by negativity, and then neglected by their caretakers. Also, it isn't just peers at school that are negatively impacting them; they are exposed to even more negativity online and on TV. Many then return to an empty home, with nobody to talk to. They feel there's no respite from the negativity surrounding them. How do they bandage their wounds and prepare for battle when there is very little triage or support? How do they become strong when their guardians play lesson thief and demand justice rather than teaching resiliency? How do they learn when guardians avoid the problem altogether by ignoring and brushing a loved one's pain under the rug because its hard to deal with or they don't have time.

Please do not mistake what we are saying about supporting your loved one if they are in a dangerous situation from being bullied at school. Of course it is important to address issues of safety with your loved ones, but it is even more important to teach them to combat bullying with the mind because it is a safe place they can retreat to.

The reality is *bullying will never go away*. It has always been here in some form or another. The people who presently bully a loved one will only bully them for a short amount of time. Middle school and high school years are very short, but very important for learning lessons. If they are not taught to be resilient today, they will find a way to overcome the painful moments of emotional abuse in other non-productive ways. If they have a home to come to where they feel safe and connected, they will be able to better cope with their problems knowing they have support. But if this lesson is not learned early, they will crumble as adults when bosses and co-workers seek them out and continue to bully them in some form or another.

Teach them when they are young that they have value and worth. Create moments where that principle can ring true over and over again. Give them the tools to properly deal with their pain. Help fill their emotional well with moments that outweigh the bad, and they will make it through. They will also go on to make it through the other times that will be tough, life changing, and insightful.

Many of you might be asking, "But, where is the line? I can't let go completely. I can't let my loved one run off the proverbial cliff they are completely blind to. I don't want my child to end up pregnant as a teen, bullied, or depressed!"

We agree. I don't think any parent or caretaker wants their loved one to make choices that could negatively impact their future. However, if your fear of these possible outcomes isn't allowing them to experience things necessary for growth, then ask yourself, "What can I let go of today that is a reflection of my fear? How can I properly support them without becoming a lesson thief, and also protect them without being a helicopter parent? Is this more about my discomfort seeing them in pain, or is there a legitimate concern here?" Once you are able to separate the two, you can see things more clearly.

Without being a lesson thief ourselves and telling you how to navigate these decisions step by step, we can suggest that if your intention is to always keep your loved one from hardship—because it's not only hard for them, but also hard for you—then you are avoiding pain. Let that be your guide, but also let your instincts as a parent or caretaker prompt you to when and where you need to be involved.

Let's go back to the image of the fierce dragon about to take out the little boy struggling to fight it. How does it feel to see someone so little trying to take down something so big? It feels scary to watch, doesn't it? You want to run and push the little boy out of the way, knowing you are double the size and have better ammunition. However, you too are alone, and that is equally as daunting. Sure, you've even killed a few dragons in your day, but you've never killed a dragon meant for someone else. Despite the fact that you think you know what you should do to win, you can't be positive because, after all, it's not your dragon. It's his or hers and it looks and acts different.

Now imagine, instead of pushing him or her out of the way, you run to his or her side with a huge container of ammunition. While he or she fights, you hold out weapon after weapon suggesting, "I don't know ... try this!"

He or she will decide to either grab that weapon, or use one of his or her own, continuing the fight until the dragon is killed. Imagine the peace that comes after a long battle is won, when he or she turns to you with familiar confidence and relief, the same you've come to enjoy over time. Your loved one won. He or she did it, and you are able celebrate that success together. That feeling is much more cohesive and more bonding than someone who pushes a loved one out of the way to save him or her.

Though he or she might feel relieved at the beginning being pushed aside, and may even thank you tremendously because he or she doesn't know how to fight yet, overtime he or she will get angrier when the dragon appears bigger and you can no longer help in the fight. Your loved one will realize that you were never truly helping, and that you were stealing the lesson, stealing your loved one's win. They will blame you and still avoid the problem because it is all they have come to know. They are truly under-prepared, and lack the courage it takes to face adversity.

PAIN, THE GREAT MOTIVATOR

The presence of pain can be an amazing teacher and motivator. It can teach you to find things you need in order to grow. We often say to teens we work with that people don't change unless change itself is less painful than the consequence. This means that when we feel the pain that comes as a consequence of our choices, we are motivated to change. If we didn't feel that pain, we wouldn't feel those consequences. Please remember this when you see a loved one going through a challenging time. It is human nature to live in joy more than pain. When a loved one is making choices that are destructive and you allow them to avoid the consequences, they don't have to feel the full weight of their consequences or the pain that it causes. They have little motivation to change. They can talk about change and convince everyone around them they will change, but it isn't until they hit rock bottom that many are finally motivated to do something different. For this purpose, pain can be a beautiful teacher throughout life—don't be afraid of it, and don't allow your loved ones to shy away as well.

The father struggling to make ends meet goes through pain, which motivates him to get out of his pain by seeking something better, like a better education or a different job. When he avoids these feelings through unhealthy coping techniques like drinking, he stunts his ability to grow. He has a choice to live a life long battle of addiction and despair or to allow the pain to motivate him to do something greater with himself.

A mother struggling with a child starts to point the finger at her struggling child because it dulls the pain of feeling inadequate. This tool of avoidance is robbing her of the opportunity to grow beyond her current ability as a mother. This pain, if she leans into it, can teach her to be a better communicator or overcome judgments she possibly acquired from her own parents. She has a choice: she can avoid and always be right, while losing those she loves, or she can stop blaming, experience the pain, and allow it to teach her how to improve her situation.

You may be concerned that we are negating certain necessary things that you should protect your loved ones from, like drug dealers, child molesters, etc. Please know that we are on board with you. There are many necessary boundaries that need to be set to properly protect your loved ones from unnecessary pain. However, we don't want you to set extreme boundaries so that you become like the fearful mother in the movie *Bubble Boy*, creating so many boundaries that your loved one does not have room to learn the lessons they need.

If you are the parent or caretaker afraid to put your child on the bus because she might be bullied, stop! If you are avoiding disciplining your loved one, though they clearly deserve it, stop! If you allow your loved one to avoid people who hurt their feelings and prevent them from resolving the situation by taking a stand in a safe and healthy way, stop! If you are doing your loved ones homework because its easier than having to deal with the complaining and frustration: stop. Stop avoiding, stop being the lesson thief, and start becoming the mentor, trainer, and coach they desperately need.

NEXT STEPS FOR MANAGING EMOTIONAL PAIN

Moving forward, it's important to address the issues of emotional pain management, not only with yourself, but also with your loved ones. You both need to deal with the way you self-medicate and handle pain or adversity. Many fail to make the connection between the hoarding mom and her child that eventually becomes addicted to pain medications. They think of it as two separate equations. We look at it as learned behaviors, observations of loved ones unable to cope with life and substituting an addiction to compensate. If what you are doing is unhealthy, stop and create a new healthy. A new healthy should not involve overindulging in things that could be unhealthy for your health or your family's well-being. This means that if you decide to pick up cycling, but become so consumed with it that you neglect your family, you have not succeeded. Take a moment to fill your resiliency tank with things you might enjoy to give you a boost, but practice living with the pain and adversity. Avoid self-medicating when something cannot be changed.

How we self-soothe or avoid discomfort and pain is incredibly important to understand. Once we are able to see ourselves clearly in regards to our patterns of avoidance, we are able to create greater understanding and acceptance within ourselves and our loved ones.

Carve out some time to talk to your loved ones about healthy strategies to deal with adversity. Apologize if you have taught unhealthy coping behaviors, and start talking about how you are changing things for the future. For families who have little children, beware of shielding your children from experiencing small challenges that they can overcome. When those challenges come, use that opportunity to talk about their discomfort, acknowledge that it is normal, and talk about ways your family will and should deal with those challenges. Create strong boundaries as to what is unacceptable in dealing with adversity, and help them to understand what the outcome will look like if they choose destructive behaviors to cope with their problems.

Ground yourself and help your loved one do the same when fantasy starts to take over their ability to move forward and deal with pain. Whenever we work with someone in this situation, they are often stuck in avoidance patterns like being apathetic or fantasizing about something that's unrealistic. It's a sign they aren't basing anything in reality and they don't know how to. Change can happen by first working to shift the thoughts that encourage the fantasy pattern. Ask yourself the following questions and teach your loved one to do the same:

- Why am I so uncomfortable?
- Why is this so painful for me?
- What am I avoiding?
- What do I get if I continue with these behaviors?
- What is another way I can deal with my discomfort, instead of falling into fantasy?
- If I don't change the way I do things, then what?

It won't be enough to just ask the questions. You must be determined to change the behavior. Fantasy addictions are similarly strong as drug addictions. When we use the example of pornography, we can understand just how powerful fantasy can be by the many examples of people who have ruined their life or relationships over their pornography addictions. A pornography addiction can take over someone's life unless they address the deeper issues attached their desire to escape from something. There could be numerous things attached to their desire to escape, like feeling shame about something in their life or that they aren't enough for someone. By understanding what those triggers are, and committing to destroying those habits, you can start to change. However, if you never address the pain associated with fantasy behaviors, things will not change. Changing long-time habits will take some time, some patience, and some understanding. It can be scary altering the way you think and see the world, so have some empathy for your loved one or yourself during the process.

For those who are stuck in fantasy land or are working with a loved one who has grandiose or unrealistic ideas about life, you can ground yourself or your loved one by asking questions like the following:

- What do you want?
- How can you get there?
- What's it going to take?
- What do you need to make this happen?
- What's your commitment level to making this happen?
- What could be some of your obstacles that could keep you from accomplishing what you want?
- How do you prevent those obstacles from derailing your goals?
- What are some realistic goals to get you there?

Questions like these will help your loved one think through some outcomes and will allow you to point them in a direction that could be more beneficial. Try not to create direction for them, but give them an opportunity to come to their own conclusions about their lifestyle. Some boundaries must be set to prevent the loved one from going back to their fantasy behavior. You will set and hold those boundaries. You'll need to ask yourself what you can do to help keep them on a productive path. Get good at asking: "Am I working towards the reality of what is going on here?" If you can't get comfortable, keep digging. We are confident you'll get to a place of peace.

Allow your loved one to set up check points, and then hold them to those check points. Don't be overbearing during this process. We like to tell people to treat their loved ones as if they were a superior at work. Treat your loved one with that same sensitivity you would show your superior, and be respectful of their space, their mind, and their emotions. You want to give your loved one enough space to figure it out, but also guide their mind so that they are grounded in more truthful information, unable to return to their fantasy cycle. You cannot change anyone; you can guide, add truth, and then repeat the process until they have made the decision to change.

Lastly, stop avoiding things that are uncomfortable, or could potentially be uncomfortable. Always remember that those you love are learning from these behaviors, and they need someone to courageously show them how to step up, be a strong individual, and deal with things that are not pleasant. Most of you already know how you avoid at this point; now, develop some self awareness, and challenge yourself and your loved ones to step up and change those patterns. Don't be afraid of the dragon. It's there to teach you, not completely destroy you. When you can understand that, it minimizes the fear of dealing with hard things.

If you can start to apply these principles and make peace with pain in your life, we know things can shift in a good way. You will find greater resiliency dealing with your challenges and your loved ones' challenges. Understanding what drives our thoughts and our behaviors when we experience pain is paramount if we want to change destructive behaviors. Remember this as you move through the next two chapters. Ask yourself how the root of pain, fear, loss, adversity, and suffering ties into the way you were conditioned to be a caretaker by your caretakers. Ask yourself how that conditioning creates a pattern of behavior that pushes your loved one further away.

REFLECTIVE POINTS & CORE PRINCIPLES TO REMEMBER

- People who become self-destructive often are overwhelmed by the presence of emotional pain. They feel they have very little support from family to cope with their loss.

- Fantasy addictions are a powerful distraction that people use to avoid pain.

- If you want to help a loved one from repetitively falling off the cliff of life, teach them how to cope in ways that are healthy. However, before you do that, make sure you teach yourself in the process.

Five

NATURE VS. NUTURE

"While genes are pivotal in establishing some aspects of emotionality, experience plays a central role in turning genes on and off. DNA is not the heart's destiny; the genetic lottery may determine the cards in your deck, but experience deals the hand you can play. Scientists have proven, for example, that good mothering can override a disadvantageous temperament."
— Thomas Lewis, A General Theory of Love

"Our first impressions are generated by our experiences and our environment, which means that we can change our first impressions... by changing the experiences that comprise those impressions."
— Malcolm Gladwell

Over the years, professionals have debated how genetics influence the outcome of a person's life versus their environment. Some believed a person's inherited genetic makeup was to blame for adverse behaviors. Others argued that a person's environment could shape their genetic expression, making it paramount to their overall wellness.

We hear caretakers debate this question as well, especially when they resist admitting that their home environment could be pushing a loved one in a direction that is unhealthy. They often claim that their loved one has tendencies and personality traits much different than their other siblings and that it's not their home environment that is pushing them over the edge; it must be genetics.

When dealing with severe personality disorders, this could be the cause. We see you, caretakers of these loved ones. However, for many of you reading today, this is not the case. Your home environment may have triggered genetically predisposed behaviors into play. Regardless of where you feel you are, all caretakers can benefit from understanding more deeply how your home environment can affect the natural tendencies of your loved ones and how genetics, when triggered by environments, can also affect the genetic expression of a young child as they grow into adulthood.

THE CHILDHOOD YEARS

In 1972, the Dunedin School of Medicine embarked on the ultimate nature vs. nurture test in what became known as The Dunedin Study. In this study, researchers followed the lives of every child born in the city of Dunedin, New Zealand that year from birth until death. Scientists documented every bit of their existence—their medical history, genetics, personality traits, habits, criminal convictions, relationships, successes and failures, drug use, jobs, relationships, etc. The significant findings from this study are now helping us better understand why some people become repeat criminal offenders, what makes a person truly violent, and why some children are more successful than others when they grow up.

Amongst the children in the study, there were five personality traits identified that remained true from the ages of three to twenty-three. They were:

1. Well-adjusted
2. Reserved
3. Inhibited
4. Under-controlled
5. Confident

Of these five personality traits, researchers estimate about twenty-eight percent of the population are the confident type, known as the "go-getters", the entrepreneurs, the ones not afraid to take on challenges. They aren't necessarily the life of the party, but they are people with a presence. Fifteen percent of the population are considered more reserved adults who are quiet and less outgoing. Forty percent of the population are estimated to be well-adjusted (the most common personality trait among the five types) and tend to be flexible and resourceful. These three personality types (well-adjusted, confident, and reserved) also tend to be more productive members of society as they mostly have positive character traits and are more likely to have friends, successful careers, be happily married, and enjoy better health throughout life.

This was not the case, however, for the other two types of personalities. The under-controlled and the inhibited types created a lot of trouble and angst for themselves and for the rest of the community. In our general population, it is estimated that seven percent of people are the inhibited type. This is the child whose shyness as an adult tends to get in the way of doing very simple things. They have a hard time leaving home and living and creating a life for themselves. They are often fearful and neurotic. They close themselves off to experiences and can be high strung as well. They are also much more prone to develop depression.

Ten percent of the general population is considered under-controlled. They are high-strung individuals, and irritable. They easily fly off the handle and they are closed off to new experiences. They don't like change in their environment, they become involved in anti-social activities, and they have a hard time in their work lives once they leave school. They are more prone to long stretches of unemployment. They also are more likely to have heart disease, diabetes, or lung problems. They are prone to anger and hostility, and at the same time they are sensation seekers. They also engage in unprotected sex and smoking at an earlier age, as well as drinking along with binging.

The Dunedin Study found that children who were slower to walk or talk often had further issues with brain development, leading to problems in adulthood. A portion of boys involved had difficulty reading and, as a result, disliked school, didn't find it engaging, and were ready to leave as soon as they could. They were also likely to do poorly in school and were later more likely to be involved in criminal activity. Something as innocent as delayed speech, if left untreated, can gather force over time and adjust the course of a child's life into adulthood.

Researchers looked at sleep patterns for children between ages five and eleven, investigating a correlation between sleep and future development. They found that children who slept the least during their early years grew up to become the most obese adults. The amount of sleep you get as a child can also predict how obese you will be by age thirty-two. This prediction was also on par with how much physical activity you do. Sleep effects the hormones that influence how hungry you feel and signal when you are full. Toddlers who slept less than normal were also more likely to have difficulty with cognitive function during adolescence and experience anxiety in their twenties.

At eleven years of age, the children were asked if they saw things or heard voices. Twenty-five years later, researchers followed up with the same children as adults. What they found was unexpected: nearly half had developed schizophrenia. Schizophrenia affects more than twenty-four million adults worldwide, but this was the first time symptoms had been recognized in children. Prior to the study results, it was assumed that the illness only existed in adults. The study found that schizophrenia doesn't begin in adult life—it is almost always preceded by developmental difficulties and minor psychotic symptoms in childhood. This groundbreaking discovery led to earlier diagnosis and intervention.

When comparing the amount of television and gaming children consumed with their overall health later in life, researchers discovered the following:

"The more TV kids watched the more likely they were to have unhealthy cholesterol levels and be cigarette smokers when they grew older. It also affected their employment prospects and their income. The amount of TV predicts how you do in school and university. The ones who watched more TV as children were three times more likely to leave school without any qualifications. The people who watched the least amount of TV were four times more likely to graduate high school and go on to to get a university degree irrespective of IQ and family income. The American academy of pediatrics now recommends parents limit TV viewing to less than two hours a day."[1]

DEVELOPING SELF-CONTROL IN CHILDREN

The Dunedin Study dug deeper. Was there anything in childhood that could predict who will or won't be successful? Does it matter if your parents are rich or poor? Does IQ matter, or is intelligence just how hard you try? Researchers found that the most powerful predictor of success in life was something else altogether.

The children who were the most successful controlling their impulses went on to have the greatest success as adults. They were entrepreneurs and good money managers. Conversely, those with impulsive behaviors were poor money managers and more likely to have things repossessed. Low levels of self-control not only predicted financial problems in adulthood, but also physical problems like obesity, high cholesterol, sexually transmitted diseases, and heart disease; they were also more likely to suffer from substance abuse addictions.

[1]"The Early Years." Predict My Future: The Story of Us, directed by Paul Casserly, Irena Dol, & Mark McNeill, Season 1, Episode 1, Razor Films, 2016.

The study revealed that self-regulation plays a very important role. The good news is that one's ability to self-control is not fixed; it can be improved. What promoted self-control and self-regulation in children was the sensitive response of parenting in infancy, followed by firm and consistent discipline, especially starting in the second and third years of life.

"It's a lot harder to change the person, than it is to change what the person does. By trying to alter a child's behavior you can change how it is that the world is responding to that child, and it doesn't mean that you are changing the child's personality, but it does mean that the child is going to be reinforced and is going to be rewarded and is going to be punished for a whole different set of behaviors."[2]

The early years are absolutely critical for how a person's life turns out. If you really want to make a difference for people when they're adults, early intervention is the key. That is where your money and your focus should go—those early years. They are seminal in all sorts of ways.

The results show that personality is set in early childhood and has lifelong consequences. Thankfully, a person's future is not a function of personality alone. The study identified something we can teach any child, no matter their personality type, that will increase their health, wealth, and happiness:

"Having a good childhood, balanced and predictable family environment where parenting is warm and sensitive and stimulating can help predict a really good life projector."[2]

Childhood is a time of hope and possibility for both caretakers and loved ones.

THE TEENAGE YEARS

During the teenage years—especially when a loved one is becoming sidetracked—it's common to begin asking how children, so innocent and full of life, can get lost along the way only to find themselves in trouble with the law and battling addiction. Researchers asked, why do teens run off the rails and what happens to them when they become adults?

The Dunedin Study found that thirteen-year-olds engaging in criminal activity were very difficult to manage as toddlers. At three years old, they ran around the room, jumped on sofas, and refused to listen to adults. If the children found a task to be frustrating, they threw things and gave up. The boys who bullied were not liked by the other children and were also

---

[2]"The Early Years." Predict My Future: The Story of Us, directed by Paul Casserly, Irena Dol, & Mark McNeill, Season 1, Episode 1, Razor Films, 2016.

more likely to engage in criminal behavior later in life.

The study allowed researchers to recognize, as early as kindergarten, which children were more likely to engage in criminal behavior if their course was not corrected. They were surprised, however, to discover that children who showed no signs of delinquency in early childhood were suddenly taking up criminal behaviors at the age of fifteen. It wasn't a few isolated teens acting up, either. A lot of teens were getting in trouble in large groups. The study showed that by the age of twenty-one, sixty percent of males had stolen property or money and seventy-five percent were involved in some form of violence. Surprisingly, almost ninety percent had abused drugs or alcohol. In the end, the Dunedin Study findings showed that teenage offending was the norm, not the exception.

"Why would well behaved kids suddenly become anti-social? Around the time of puberty, there's an increase of sensation seeking, novelty seeking, and reward seeking. This is natural and normative and impels people towards more exciting behaviors. This thirst for excitement is reflective in car crash studies where teens are four times more likely to be in a car crash; and if there are other teens in the car, the risk of the crash being fatal doubles. Other types of accidents follow the same pattern, including drowning. They just take more chances.

"We think the reason for this is what is going on in the adolescent brain, which is a work of progress; it is being rewired and restructured. The changes start at the back for the brain, and the part of the brain responsible for judgements and self-control are at the front of the brain and are rewired last. This makes teens prone to risky and reckless behavior. They focus on the present and fail to think about possible long-term consequences. The front of their brain isn't working yet."[3]

Every caretaker's nightmare is that their wayward teen will end up in jail. The study showed, as teen offenders get older, they separate into two very distinct groups. The first is the teen who wants to try everything as an adolescent. They get involved in delinquent acts and drug use as part of exploring what life is all about. The second is the teen who showed aggression and bullying behaviors from early childhood. They were shown to continue their negative behaviors into their late thirties and go on to have serious careers in crime.

The group of teens who kept offending as adults were the same children identified as potential criminals in kindergarten. The study labeled them as "life course persistent offenders" because in each stage of life, they picked

[3]"When Teens Run Off The Rails." Predict My Future: The Story of Us, directed by Paul Casserly, Irena Dol, & Mark McNeill, Season 1, Episode 2, Razor Films, 2016.

up anti-social behaviors. For example, when they got a driver's license, they began to steal cars; when they got their first job, they began to embezzle money; when they had a girlfriend, they would abuse her. Their anti-social behavior persisted throughout their life course. The children who were often disruptive or loud, acted like a clown, picked on people, and struggled to maintain focus grew to abuse drugs and increase in the severity of their crimes from petty theft to armed robbery.

The majority of teen offenders studied were found to stop offending by their mid-twenties; they were labeled as "adolescent limited offenders." These were those ordinary, healthy teens that would act out a bit and get into a little trouble, but they didn't have difficult temperaments or verbal skill problems. They would course correct in their own time unless they were too deeply imbedded in their own criminal lifestyle. Three things the study found that teens had the most difficulty coming out of as adults were drugs, gangs, and jail.

TEENAGE GIRLS

Teenage girls were found to also offend, with ninety-one percent of the girls committing increased delinquent behavior before the age of twenty-one. However, the study found that these girls went off the rails earlier than the boys. The teenage girls who went through puberty early now looked like adults, making them especially vulnerable because of the widened gap between their appearance and their developing cognitive function. Attractive, intellectually immature girls got into a lot of trouble. This phenomenon didn't appear with the boys. When girls became sexually active, researchers asked what kind of partner the girls were attracted to. The girls reported wanting someone with a personality like their own. If they were sensation-seeking, so was their partner; if they were conscientious, so was their partner. The similarities even came down to the reading level if there was a disability. Ultimately, researchers found that delinquent women seek out equally delinquent men who were just as anti-social and in trouble with the law as they were.

In the study, most teen girls' delinquency and anti-social behavior was a passing phase. The exceptions were girls experiencing teen pregnancy (and consequently missing out on education), girls becoming single mothers, and girls struggling with money. These teen girls are prone to developing addictions in an attempt to cope with the pain of their situations.

Females who picked relationships with males who were neurotic and lacked the ability to be agreeable, having what they called "negative emotionality," would eventually find themselves in a physically violent relationship. Researchers found that in such relationships, females hit males just as often as males hit females. When questioned why they hit, the females felt it was not wrong if they hit their partner, because they didn't feel they would seriously injure anyone in doing so; whereas when a male hits a female, she is more likely to end up in the hospital. These findings were quite controversial when they were released and, subsequently, many female criminologists rejected the findings.

THE BEST COURSE OF ACTION FOR TEEN OFFENDERS

"When a teen is caught offending, it is often tough to know what the best course of action is. We, in the past as a society, may have been dealing with teen delinquency in a way that, over time, was more harmful by incarcerating teens rather than putting into place systems that would rehabilitate and/or manage a teen outside of the juvenile detention facilities. The question must be asked then, when a teen is presented in front of the courts, which path are they on? Because the teen that is going to grow out of it—you wouldn't want to give them a prison record that would stop them from getting a job and retard their natural assistance in crime."[4]

The Dunedin Study found that teen offenders who are sent to prison are far more likely to be offenders as adults than teens who committed similar offenses but weren't sent to jail. The New Zealand prison system recognizes this fact and gives juvenile offenders a chance to correct their course. The overall hope is to buy time for the teens' brains to catch up.

In the United States, adolescent offenders have often been treated like adult offenders, receiving harsh adult sentences. This keeps teens in the system, turning them into "lifers" who would otherwise probably course correct and go on to becoming a healthy, law-abiding citizen as an adult. Since teens lack the ability to plan and think ahead or regulate their emotions and behaviors, they are less capable of stopping themselves from acting on their impulses. Ninety-five percent of all juvenile offenders do not go on to commit multiple crimes, so why don't we treat them like they do in New Zealand and give juveniles a chance to correct course? By doing so, we would increase our troubled teens' chances of getting out of the system and leading healthy, productive lives.

In 2010, the U.S. Supreme Court agreed with the findings from The Dunedin Study and removed the death sentence for teens, resulting in the

---

[4]"When Teens Run Off The Rails." Predict My Future: The Story of Us, directed by Paul Casserly, Irena Dol, & Mark McNeill, Season 1, Episode 2, Razor Films, 2016.

moving of seventy-two teen offenders off Death Row. But even with this change, we still have far to go. Given that ten percent of criminals are responsible for fifty percent of all crime, is it possible to do something about proven repeat offenders? According to researchers, "It's very difficult, but not impossible. But the key is prevention rather than treatment. So many teens show signs even before they get in trouble with the law. And by not dealing with that in that moment in time, we may be missing opportunities to prevent a lifetime of chronic anti-social behavior. It's possible to turn an adolescent limited offender's life around, but it's a lot harder for a life course persistent offender."[5]

Helping teens escape a life of delinquency starts by giving them privileges and responsibilities that are age appropriate. In doing so, we give them a stake in their own lives. The irony, then, is that teens will begin to think about the life and legacy they want to build—which is completely opposite from the way they were living their lives when they were making delinquent choices. This is often hard for caretakers to do—to let go of the reins and allow their loved ones to find their own path and sometimes, if not often, stumble into obstacles in their way. But the lessons they learn during these times, with you as their coach, guiding them over and around obstacles and cheering them on as they go, these lessons are invaluable in helping them succeed as adults in the future.

WHAT OUR GENES ARE TELLING US TODAY

When we first set out to understand nature vs. nurture, we often had conversations about loved ones who were repeat offenders, or those who just couldn't get themselves on the right path, no matter how hard they tried. It was as if they would do well for some time, and then they'd be back in a relapsed state. This can be devastating for any caretaker or supporting person who has invested much time, money, and energy into helping their loved one.

As we began helping families search for answers, some would stumble upon diagnoses that would explain a struggling loved one's predicament such as BPD (bipolar disorder or borderline personality disorder), anxiety disorders, chronic depression, etc. In the past, very few understood on a deeper level what genetic inheritances were also working against them. Thanks to The Dunedin Study, that understanding has been brought to light.

The study found that almost all violent adults had something similar in

---

[4]"When Teens Run Off The Rails." Predict My Future: The Story of Us, directed by Paul Casserly, Irena Dol, & Mark McNeill, Season 1, Episode 2, Razor Films, 2016.

their upbringing: a history of maltreatment and neglect before age eleven. While abused children were more likely to become violent criminals, abuse wasn't a definitive factor in predicting violence in adults. Many abused children grow up to be normal members of society.

Another commonality found amongst violent men was a missing or weaker MAOA gene. The MAOA gene is found in every human on the planet. It regulates the hormones that effect a person's mood and behaviors. It also affects one's response to stress. Thirty percent of the population have missing or weakened versions of MAOA, but the majority are not violent people. It's special environmental circumstance, nurture—or the lack of it—that causes that weak or missing MAOA gene to express itself in the form of aggressive and violent behavior.

Like humans, rhesus monkeys also carry the MAOA genotype. Studies done by the National Institute of Health (NIH) showed that monkeys with weaker MAOA genes created chaos amongst other monkeys who, in return, would treat their disruptive behavior with disdain. This would lead to more frequent and escalating anti-social until the largest male would step in to beat them back. This confrontation would ignite even more anger in the monkeys with low MAOA, resulting in a face-to-face confrontation with the largest male. These aggressive males get kicked out of their troops at an early age because their behavior is not tolerated. Without a troop, they typically perish within a year.

So, what is it that creates violent people and repeat offenders? The Dunedin Study predicts that maltreatment, combined with weak or missing MAOA, will result in an outcome of violent behavior. "It was as if nature loaded the gun, but nurture pulled the trigger."[6]

What then happens to someone born with weak or missing MAOA but who grows up in a good home environment? Professor James Fallon has been researching the criminal mind and the MAOA gene for years. While studying the brain patterns of criminals, he decided to scan his own brain and found that his brain looked just like those of the violent criminals. Genetic testing confirmed that Fallon had the MAOA gene deletion. His brain pattern reflected someone impulsive, aggressive, and violent.

"By looking at my brain you would think I would be in jail," Fallon remarked. In fact, there are seven convicted murderers in his family tree. But regardless of his genetics and family history, Professor Fallon is not a violent person. He attributes this solely to the supportive and loving upbringing his parents gave him as a child. Again, we see how a nurturing

---

[6]"When Genes Mix With The Wrong Environment." Predict My Future: The Story of Us, directed by Paul Casserly, Irena Dol, & Mark McNeill, Season 1, Episode 3, Razor Films, 2016.

home environment is crucial in helping people, regardless of their genetic predisposition, to find greater success in life.

5-HTT SEROTONIN TRANSPORTER GENE AND DEPRESSION

Billions of dollars are spent yearly treating depression in the United States. Although a depressive episode is a normal response to difficult circumstances, many teens and adults are struggling to bounce back from them. It is believed now that depression might be another genetic expression triggered by environmental factors like stress.

Cue the 5-HTT serotonin transporter gene. It comes in long or short form. When those with the longer transporter gene experience stress, they could either develop a depressive episode that might come and go, or they could get through their adversity completely unscathed. Those with the shorter version could potentially become clinically depressed and/or suicidal when faced with a stressful environment. However, according to the Dunedin Study, this more severe reaction only presented itself in short 5-HTT carriers who had either been mistreated as children or who experienced adversity as adults.

The NIH found identical reactions in monkeys, both in terms of behavioral characteristics of depression and withdrawal. This proved that environment could change the way genes express themselves. Genes don't have fixed outcomes, but they can be activated or switched on by events in people's lives. It's no longer an argument of nature vs. nurture. How the plant turns out is not simply determined by what was in its seed to begin with; it is the environment around the seed that determines how successfully it will grow into the plant it could become.

HOW SUBSTANCES AFFECT GENE EXPRESSION

The Dunedin Study proved the connection between one's environment and their genetic expression. Researchers wondered, could substance use have the same affect? They decided to do a deep dive on cannabis, a commonly used recreational drug amongst both teens and adults. What researchers found might surprise you.

One in one hundred people suffer from schizophrenia. Schizophrenia and other psychoses can develop when a deletion of the CMOT gene occurs. In the study, ten percent of participants who used cannabis in their teens ended up developing schizophrenia. This is ten times the expected rate. Researchers also observed that participants with a deletion of the CMOT gene were more likely to develop psychosis if they were heavy cannabis users before the age of fifteen. Participants with the gene deletion who used cannabis as adults were not affected.

The study also showed that cannabis use affects intelligence:

"Most people are told that their IQ is stable and that once you reach fifteen, it doesn't get any better. But that is not quite true—there is quite a bit of change. Cannabis disrupted the growing brain. The study members with long term use had lost IQ points. Not everyone lost IQ points. The ones who lost most were the ones who started very early in life, when they were around thirteen to fifteen years old. Users using before the age of eighteen lost an average of eight IQ points, and the IQ loss appears to be permanent. Eight IQ points is the difference between a fishing villager and a fishing boat owner; the different between a dental hygienist and a dentist. So, it does have a big association between the kind of work people are able to master. Better memory and intellectual performance, stronger attention, helps you get further in education."[7]

Teens who use cannabis daily and become dependent on cannabis, are less likely to graduate high school, and have higher rates of suicide. They need to be made aware of the potential harm of using cannabis before adulthood. There's a widespread belief that using cannabis is like using alcohol or cigarettes—no big deal. But considering both the short- and long-term mental health risks, teens using cannabis is a very big deal.

THE WRAP UP

It is true that because of our genetic makeup, we are more susceptible to adversity. But how fascinating and intriguing is it that those same genes make us more likely to benefit from positive environmental influences and enrichment? In other words, our genes are malleable on the upside and, as a result, the same genes that make us vulnerable can turn us into lucky people when things go well.

So, what at first glance might look like bad genes, could be good genes for some people in the right circumstances. Dr. James Fallon thinks he might be one of those people. If you looked only at his genetic make-up, the prediction would be that he was a very aggressive and anti-social person. "I have a lot of characteristics that people with these combos have, but I'm not a criminal. Haven't been in jail. I've been a good boy, but I'm very

[7]"When Genes Mix With The Wrong Environment." Predict My Future: The Story of Us, directed by Paul Casserly, Irena Dol, & Mark McNeill, Season 1, Episode 3, Razor Films, 2016.

aggressive. And I hate to lose; and I just turn it into winning everything I possibly can."

The same amygdala excitability that is associated with the short form 5-HTT serotonin transporter gene in depression can be detrimental if you have a lot of stress in your life; but if you have nurturing and supportive friends and family, that same excitability can be very beneficial. The Dunedin Study suggests you may be more proactive, more empathic towards individuals, more responsive to the needs of others, and more socially responsible.

Just knowing someone carries a gene doesn't tell us very much. It's the environment that person is raised in that we should be focusing our energies on. We can help turn on and off the context of these genes merely by the environment we provide for our loved ones to grow up in.

The best thing society can do is help parents be good parents and give them the support they need. Because the lesson is clear: no matter what genes you have, a positive upbringing will benefit anyone. And a safe and happy childhood is the best foundation for a happy life.

Learning how you have been conditioned to be the caretaker you are, and how your upbringing has shaped the many layers of programming you subconsciously or consciously use to parent is where we start next.

REFLECTIVE POINTS & CORE PRINCIPLES TO REMEMBER:

- Although some children are born into this life with predisposed character traits that can negatively impact their development, much of this is determined by the environment they are raised in. Understanding your roll as caretakers in the nurture vs. nature argument gives you more power to help shape the life of your loved one because no outcome is determined by genes alone.

- Almost all teens break the law at some point; some will get caught and some will not. There are two types of offenders: those who, given the chance, will stop on their own accord; and those who will continue to break the law. Society can do a lot to recognize the difference and give wayward teens a chance to grow up rather than automatically sending them to jail. This doesn't mean there shouldn't be punishment for criminal activity; but for most teen offenders, jobs, relationships, and families will be reasons enough to give up a life of crime.

- The good news is the Dunedin Study has shown that the vast majority of those who break the law are not a threat to society. They don't need prison time. They need help growing out of delinquency. Given the proper support, they will come right, contribute to the economy, raise families, and become good citizens.

- When considering your loved one and some of the triggers they may have regarding their mental state, it's important to ask yourself these questions: What is my home environment and parenting style doing for this particular child? Am I triggering predisposed tendencies by being overly anxious or stressed? Am I recognizing personality traits that need further positive development? Am I talking to the right people who can help me understand the depth of the situation I am facing?

- In the end, the most important thing to take away from this chapter is an understanding that there is always more runway at home with your loved ones than you realize. Treatment outside of the home is sometimes necessary, but more than you would suspect, when the home environment is addressed, much of what troubles our loved ones can also be effectively remedied.

Six

PEELING BACK THE ONION

"Every chef has a technique for dealing with an onion. It causes discomfort, pain, maybe even some tears. But in the end, the onion needs to be dealt with."

—Unknown

Imagine for one moment that you're holding a golden yellow onion. Take a knife and carefully peel off the protective skin around the onion. Now, with your hands, start to pull back the layers of the onion. Notice the veins and the unique features in every layer, and how each layer is protecting the core. Compare yourself to that onion, with your unique layers representing your personality, style, habits, beliefs, behaviors, dreams, and expectations, all pointing to the core of who you are.

Now, think of your loved ones. If you were to peel back their layers, what things would you have in common? What have they learned from you, that you learned from your caretakers? How might that be getting in the way with how you connect?

As caretakers, you have been conditioned over time to be who you are today. Much of how you act and react around a loved one is a reflection of those habits, beliefs, communication styles, and conflict-resolution techniques. Your loved one is learning from you as well, watching and observing every facial expression, tone, and attitude. All of this is being recorded at their subconscious level. If you overeat to make yourself happy, they most likely will learn to deflect their discomfort and find a vice to comfort themselves. If you yell and scream in conflict, lose your cool or get frustrated easily, they learn that it's okay to do the same.

> I noticed my youngest son was spiraling downward at home and at school. He wouldn't open up and talk about it either. After working with a therapist, I learned that his behavior was a reflection of his belief about who he was. Over the last year, he felt berated and attacked by the way I would often yell at him for not doing what I told him to do. To protect himself, he learned to yell back, and that got him into more trouble with me. Then he was angry that I could yell, but he couldn't, so he eventually just gave up. Now instead of exploding, he was boiling inside and it would come out in disturbing ways. I wanted to blame him for his actions. I wanted to make him the problem, but I had to learn I was a trigger to the explosion. I was a part of the problem.
>
> —Hannah

When caretakers with struggling loved ones approach us, they are overwhelmed with their loved ones' negative behaviors and reactions. They will often point out their behaviors as being unacceptable or frightening, like addictions, disrespect, violence, passive-aggressive attitudes, withdrawal, and more. When we ask them to consider how their loved ones might have learned or accepted this type of behavior, we are met with blank stares. Most of the time, influences outside of the home are blamed, but very rarely do they take responsibility or make any connection between their behaviors and that of their loved ones. In essence, they are unable to peel back the layers of their onion and take a closer look.

Why do caretakers refuse to take responsibility? Most often it is because if they do, it means greater responsibility and ownership of their own actions. It means they are part of the problem, which is painful and uncomfortable to accept. Like we learned in Chapter 4, if we avoid our own pain, it's natural to avoid the truth that we are co-creators in our loved ones' breakdowns as well.

DISSECTING YOUR LAYERS

Your layers of conditioning are a reflection of beliefs you have about the way things should be, how people should react and behave, vows you've made to yourself about what you would change when you become a caretaker, ways you behave based on your fears from your past, your overall belief about the world, how you show up for your loved ones, and how you expect your loved ones to show up as well.

So, what are the layers that might be adding some negative weight to your relationship? If your loved one has been watching everything you say and do, how could that create a problem in your life? Take a moment to think about all of the distasteful behaviors your loved one has. Next, think how you too might be guilty of the same type of behavior. If they lie, when have you possibly lied in front of them or bent the truth? If they are addicted to something, how have you shown them that you use addictions to solve your discomfort? If they are lazy, when have you allowed them to be lazy? If they use you, how have you failed to set appropriate boundaries or have continued to enable them?

Are there beliefs you have that cause conflict between you and a loved one? Are there vows you've made in the past that you haven't kept or can't keep?

> I grew up in a home that was very poor. We didn't have enough money for food sometimes, and I was always wearing hand-me-down clothes from friends and family. They were always outdated and worn. I started to feel really self-conscious about what I was wearing, especially when the girls at school started to laugh and point, whispering behind my back. I felt alone and scared. Even though I loved my caretakers, I felt angry with them that they brought us into the world when they couldn't afford it. I vowed in my mind that I would never make my loved ones go through what I went through. Fast forward twenty years and I have two children of my own. We are a busy family like most, and we are having some problems with my eldest son. He's lived quite the charmed life, and unfortunately I'm learning that I never made him work for anything. I am learning that the unresolved pain from my past and my vow to never make him suffer the way I did has gotten in the way. Now I've got an even bigger problem on my hands because he has an attitude of entitlement—one that I allowed him to have.
>
> —Christina

> I remember my next-door neighbors were real screw ups. My mom says that it was because their kids had too much time on their hands. I vowed then that my kids would not end up that way, so I now have them on a pretty tight schedule. I am that kind of mom. Everything was going well until this last year, when my loved one started pulling crazy stuff on me. It's like he's a totally different person, and he doesn't want to do anything. This of course makes me afraid because I can see him being just like the kids next door, so I keep pushing and pushing. I'm getting

nowhere. I'm about ready to give up and give in, but my fear keeps me in the game."

—Sylvie

Could there be behaviors you unknowingly picked up from your care-takers in the way you resolve problems or how you parent a loved one? Here are a couple of examples.

We didn't really talk about things in my house. We watched a lot of television and just did our own thing, I guess. I can remember feeling like it would have been nice to be like some of the other families I saw or heard about who had dinner together, or went on vacations together. If we did anything like that, I'd be shocked. Now that I have my own family, I hate to admit it, but I don't spend too much time talking to them either. In fact, I don't think I know how to even if I tried. So I just do my own thing, and trust that it will all work out okay, like it did for me.

—Ben

I find myself always picking myself and the people around me apart. It's like I can't turn off the criticism in my mind. In the car, I've always got a comment to say about someone who's passing by. When my loved ones say mean things about people, I get really mad at them, but then they get mad at me. But it's different when I make the comments. I only make comments about people to show them what they shouldn't do with their lives, not to make fun of them like my loved ones do. When I was asked to think about where I started to learn to be so critical, I realized my caretaker and my friends were exactly the same way. Not that I am blaming them, but that's what we did everyday . . . talk about other people and criticize them.

—Alice

Can you see any correlation between who you are and the way you have conflicts with your loved one? Do you recognize the way they are currently mirroring you?

My caretaker struggled to tell people 'no' when they asked her for favors or commitments to things that she neither had enough time or resources for. This lifestyle became complicated when it put her family on the back burner and extended her energy far beyond what she knew she had. She began to be short and tired with us, and we were getting less of her than what she had ever intended. As I grew into my teenage years, I overextended myself as well, unable to say no to anyone. I remember my caretaker being incredibly frustrated that I didn't have time to do the things she needed me to do for her. I found myself pulled in a world where I couldn't please anyone, so I just gave up.

—Caroline

My caretaker's crutch was control. It made them feel safe in thinking that they could prevent their loved ones from making as many mistakes as possible by using control. It was confusing for them then when I developed an eating disorder. My eating disorder in their mind had nothing to do with control. It wasn't until therapy that my caretakers realized how my need to control what I ate was a mirror to their need to control. Once they were able to let go of control, I slowly started to let go of my need to as well.

—Elizabeth

My caretaker came from a family that yelled all the time. When I was younger, I felt scared when my parents would yell. When I started to get older, I reacted to their anger. It was like World War III at the house. When a counselor helped us address the way we dealt with conflict, where our issues originated from, what purpose they were serving, and how to reprogram the way we were reacting, we could hear each other more clearly. The fighting started to subside little by little, and we were on our way to healing.

—Joshua

I am a conflict avoider. I don't like to deal with things that make me uncomfortable. This is starting to show up in the lives of my loved ones as well. They avoid doing anything that makes them feel uncomfortable: chores, calling on a job they may not get, applying for college, etc. Their creative avoidance stems from my need to avoid. I haven't taught them otherwise, so I guess I shouldn't be so surprised.

—Harold

We noticed a relationship between a mother and daughter where the mother was overbearing and controlling. The daughter responded with insecurity in making choices, an inability to solve problems, and passive behaviors when people angered her. Her mother had been solving her problems as a way to control her environment for years, and when the daughter had a conflict, she would run to her mom to make it better.

When the daughter ended up in coaching, she struggled to ask for what she wanted, express herself, and step into her own groove. The daughter finally admitted that she struggled in her own relationship with her husband. She would control him by being passive aggressive, by storming off when she was upset, and by never allowing herself to open up. She was in fact mirroring her mother's behaviors in very different ways. Where the mother was verbally overbearing and controlling, the daughter was passive about her ways of manipulating and controlling in order to get what she wanted. When she made the connection as to why she had developed those layers of her personality, she was able to address them more effectively and change.

There are a myriad of ways your loved ones mirror the layers of conditioning you obtained in your youth. Since this mirroring can be subtle, it can often go undetected. When the mirroring goes undetected and a loved one starts clashing with their caretaker, the caretaker may start to look for answers. This is the time where shame, frustration, fear, anger, and pain invite blame into the game. The *we* switches to *you*, which pushes the struggling loved one—conditioned to be exactly what you allowed them to be—further away. This creates anger, distrust, and distance between the caretaker and the loved one. You may not be responsible for every bad decision your loved one has made or could make, but you are responsible for your own conditioning, how you project that in a negative way, and how you allow that conditioning to perpetuate in your loved one.

Detecting a correlation between the way your loved ones behave and your behaviors can be tricky to understand, especially when much of what they do isn't identical to what you do. In order to understand, you need to dig deep to see how your loved one has used your behaviors in their life, and how they adjusted and twisted what they learned.

We remember working with a client whose father was so upset that his son would continue to tell little white lies or try to distract his father from the truth until he ultimately found out. Each time the teen would tell these little lies and get caught, he would receive some type of punishment for it, like losing rights to the car. As we worked with the teen, of his levels of self-destruction came from his frustration that all of his rights were gone. When we asked him why he lied, he said:

"I didn't lie, I just didn't tell the truth . . . I didn't tell him about where I was because I knew he would be mad. He overreacts and assumes I'm doing something I shouldn't, so I didn't want the drama. My dad is such a hypocrite sometimes because a few weeks ago when we were having a good day, he told me something about his health that I thought was pretty bad. He then told me not to tell mom because he didn't want to worry her. When she asked about his appointment, he just told her things were going to be okay. He didn't really tell her the truth either. He didn't really tell my mom the truth, so I didn't think it was wrong to worry him when I said I was going somewhere I wasn't, because I knew it wouldn't be a big deal, and he would have made it a big deal."

In this example, we see how the subtle, well-intended behaviors of the father affected the son. These behaviors taught the son that holding back information that might worry or hurt loved ones was okay.

Isn't it ironic that this father became offended, upset, and disconnected with his son when he mirrored his actions? When the father became angry, his son felt betrayed and misjudged, and disconnected from his father.

"Where was his punishment?" thought the son. When we pointed this out to the father, we were met with story after story validating his point of view and blaming his teen. He couldn't accept his part in creating the situation he hated. In order to really help this father and son grow together, we needed the father to first admit his wrongs. If this father had taken the time to acknowledge his part in the breakdown of the relationship, we could have helped the two of them. Instead, they both went on defending their position and the relationship continued to self-destruct.

What subtleties are you missing? How might you be afraid or unwilling to acknowledge your loved one's negative reactions? Can you see how their reactions are similar to yours? Here is a list of additional questions to help you dissect what could be adding to your conflict with your loved ones:

- If my loved one self-medicates by using harmful substances, in what way may I self-medicate when I'm unhappy?

- If my loved one is struggling with their sexual identity and I don't understand them, in what way does my behavior drive them away from me?

- If my loved one thinks I am always critical of them, in what way am I critical of myself or others around me? In what way were those around me critical when I was younger?

- If my loved one has a problem controlling their anger, in what way may I be allowing them to act out? Do I show them that it's okay to not control your anger when you are mad?

- If my loved one avoids the pain of interaction or doing

hard tasks, in what way do I procrastinate doing the things I should do?

- If my loved one shuts down when we try and talk about problems, in what way might I shut down with others when I feel forced to talk about things I don't want to talk about?

- If my loved one is overly sexual with another person and is seeking attention and validation, in what ways do I do the same? In what ways might I not be spending enough time helping my loved one build a better sense of self-worth?

- If my loved one feels like I favor other children, in what ways might I have experienced this myself and could be doing the same thing to them?

For those of you who may not relate to the particular scenarios and questions we just posed, here are a few simple questions where you can fill in the blank to help get closer to your current reality:

- If my loved one is _____, then in what way could I be making the problem worse?

- If my loved one is _____, then how does it make me feel about me, and what do I do to protect myself from feeling that way?

- If my loved one is _____, how do I self-medicate to keep myself from feeling the pain I do?

- If my loved one is _____, in what way do I try and hide it from others, and how is that affecting my family and me today?

- If my loved one is _____, what do I fear most based on what I've experienced in my past?

- If my loved one is _____, what part of our family situation causes pain and makes me feel completely unsettled? What do you think your loved one would say, and how might they be dealing with that in a negative way?

- If my loved one is_____,
  explain what I think might cause instability, lost hope, and
  uncertainty in their lives.

- If my loved one is _____,
  how do I try to control the situation, and how is that affecting our relationship?

After honestly asking yourself these questions, do you think you may be involved in how your loved one is reacting? Do you see how you could be part of the problem? Could it be time to talk to someone who can help you work through some problems, so you can build the relationship you want? If you don't learn how to do things differently, how will you know how to direct your loved one to do the same? A teacher cannot teach math if they don't know how to solve the equation. You likewise cannot teach a loved one to change if you don't know how to change yourself.

> My mom grew up in an environment where there was a lot of judgment, fear, and criticism. It was only natural when she started her family that she used what she learned from her family with her own children. All of her kids seemed to cope and deal with her parenting except for one, who liked to question everything. I'm sure some of you have loved ones like that. Maybe it was a little scary for her because it challenged the layers of who she was and how things had been done. The more the layers were pulled back, the more her need for control was discovered. The more control she used, the more crippled the relationship became. When she became self aware of her past and worked with someone who helped her, she was able to gain the relationship she wanted. She was able to see more clearly how she could help me as well.
>
> —Jonathan

Understanding your layers of conditioning and the why and how we do what we do with loved ones is the best way to learn what could be going on with your loved ones and why they react the way they do. Remember, the pathway to healing a connection is brick by brick. Accepting a brick into your relationship's infrastructure does not ensure all will be well, but without it, your foundation will be weaker.

THE UNFAMILIAR LAYER

It isn't uncommon to listen to a caretaker truthfully express how completely bizarre and different their loved ones' behaviors are in comparison to the behaviors they should have learned in their home environment. These caretakers typically have worked to peel back the layers of their own conditioning and heal what needs to be healed. Despite that, their loved ones show signs of conditioning that don't reflect what the caretakers felt they have taught or emulated in their relationships. When they approach us trying to understand how they can change or what they might have done wrong, we offer this bit of insight.

There are two scenarios where struggling loved ones born to healthy caretakers continue to struggle despite the best efforts of the caretaker. Some caretakers have loved ones struggling with emotional or mental disorders, like Asperger's, Autism, Multiple Personality Disorder, or other mental illnesses. Others have loved ones that, unbeknown to their caretaker or mentor, have misunderstood or misjudged their caretakers' intentions, beliefs, or conditioning and have created personal beliefs about themselves that are false and secret from their caretakers.

For those dealing with someone who has a mental or emotional disorder, this concept of healing past conditioning and mirroring behaviors may not be as effective as quickly as it would with someone who has a loved one without a disorder. This doesn't mean that what we are teaching you isn't of some importance or relevant to you, but it just means that even if you master this technique, your loved one could continue to battle merely because of their inability to respond normally. In these cases, you and your loved one will need the added skill set of someone who can further help, like someone trained to help those with mental or emotional disorders. Being realistic about this scenario can help you focus your attention on things that can really help, rather than beating yourself up over your inability to see or direct change in your loved one.

The second following scenario involves a loved one who has at some point inadvertently accepted truth and conditioning from your behaviors that in no way reflect your core beliefs. Here is an example of this type of scenario:

I remember watching my mom put on make-up before going to a party. She made the comment that her dress was getting too small, and I remember the look of disgust on her face as she tried to adjust the dress. I felt sad and ashamed for her. I didn't want to feel that way myself, so I vowed to never get fat. A few years later into my teen years, my mother was noticing I was micromanaging everything regarding my weight, my looks, my photos on social media, my clothing, and more. Everything was revolving around my need to be perfect. I was protecting myself, but she was concerned. When we were in coaching, I shared this experience and admitted that this moment was pivotal for me and was why I was acting the way I was. It wasn't only her, but after that I started to notice things all around me that said "I was right," which just intensified my convictions. When the coach met with my mom she admitted to remembering that moment, but the thing that went through her mind at that time was not that she was ashamed of herself, but that she was bothered that she would have to buy another dress, and didn't want to spend the money. Later I learned that my perception of that moment was false, and what I chose to invest in—the conditioning I created—was a reflection of my belief based on my perception.

—Dana

This happens to many people and possibly has happened to each and everyone one of us at some point in our lives. You can never completely control how your loved one perceives some of the ways you act or behave. When a loved one is younger, he or she is often limited by his or her ability to reason, to understand consequence, or equate expressions or motives. Because of this, he or she will decide how things add up with his or her limited understanding of the world.

At times, this can feel unnerving, especially to those who want to believe that if you are aware enough, you can prevent most wrongdoings from happening to your loved one. No matter how perfect you are, you cannot control how others perceive the world in which they live. Do not be discouraged. As long as you are willing to communicate, detect things early on, and invest in a healthy and communicative relationship—one where you can talk about things you observe in your loved one's life—you can head off a false belief and redirect a loved one easily.

When I noticed that my loved one was developing low self-esteem, I was confused. We had always affirmed her positively, so I thought, "Where was this coming from?" Little did I know that that one time her father couldn't attend an event she felt was very special to her, she felt ashamed and unloved. This was her new truth despite all the thousands of other moments we showed her we loved her and validated her. All it took was this one time for her perception to shift and the negativity started to seep in slowly. When we were able to come to terms with that, apologize, and help her create a more truthful reality, she started to perform better, and we were on our way to healing.

—Bella

GOLD PLATING THE ONION

It is no easy task to sit back and reflect on how you became a co-creator in your current crisis with your loved one. Many don't want to deal with the onion. They would rather leave the tough protective skin on and dissect everyone else but themselves. We call this "gold plating the onion."

Gold plating the onion is dangerous in the game of connection. It creates shame in the eyes of your loved ones when they don't feel like they can make you happy, and that they are always wrong, broken, or messed up. On a subconscious level, it is also very confusing for them. How can they be wrong and you be right? In their mind, they are doing exactly as they have seen you do. This confusion leads to anger, which leads to the need to self-soothe, which is what often gets them into trouble when they turn to things or others that are destructive.

In all the years working in and around treatment centers, we saw a pattern emerge that solidified our belief in how people gold plate the onion. Sending a loved one to treatment is taxing both emotionally and financially. The pattern is as follows:

A new loved one comes and gets settled in. He is in shock. The first family therapy session comes around with a laundry list of grievances and things to change, and the weight of the world rests on the loved one's shoulders. With time, the therapist learns more about the parents and the therapist begin to see the gold plating. At first, the therapist is bombarded with statements like, "All my other kids turned out fine," and "We've been nothing but patient." Eventually, the truth emerges, and we start to hear, "Well, when they change, I will change," or "I'm not paying you to help me, I'm paying to you help my son/daughter." All of these are further signs of gold plating the onion: that the mutuality of their relationship does not exist, and that dealing with their own personal discomfort is too difficult. Then the caretaker will place conditions on their loved one in order for the loved one to be in the caretaker's good graces again. This then conditions the loved one to negotiate what he must give away in order to survive, to appease, or to be heard.

My caretaker could never accept they were wrong. I lost a part of myself by accepting that I always was the bad guy. I had to give in to survive. Giving in meant I started to feel like I was a worthless piece of garbage.

Then I started to do things on purpose that would make me earn that title.

—Michael

Questioning my sexuality seemed to put my caretakers into cardiac arrest. Instead of helping me accept and deal with how I was feeling, I was fighting their conditions about the way I had to think. Hiding myself more and more every day, feeling devastated that I couldn't meet up to their beliefs and expectations . . . this is when I lost myself.

—Adam

Them versus us becomes so commonplace in this world. Do this and I will be happy, or change this and I'll know you care. The gold plating makes you deflect. The brilliant shine of the onion is false, just like the father who held back information from his wife and who conditioned his son to do the same. It was hard for him to admit that he needed to change. His gold plating mentality only allowed him to see himself as right and perfectly justified. He was deceived, and they both suffered.

Beware that accepting your part in conflict can sometimes interfere with past programming or conditioning. It can almost feel as if someone is telling you the color red is no longer red. After believing the color red has been red for 30 years, you have to contradict everything you know to be real and true. To keep you from feeling this discomfort and confusion, you might say, "I don't need to change . . . no, I mean, I *really* don't need to change!"

Be aware that caretakers might avoid taking ownership by creating alternate scenarios—like the below examples—by sharing these alternate realities with friends and family to receive approval.

My other children are perfectly fine, it's this one who has decided to make poor choices. If I was the problem, I think my other children would have problems too.

—Jamie

You might also say, "It's not my fault things are bad. I'm at work all day. This is my wife's department," or "I never abused drugs. Why would I be responsible for their choices?" Meanwhile, packages from FedEx might be piling up at the door from a late night shopping addiction or you may be overindulging in food, alcohol, or other common addictions. This is how you gold-plate the onion.

We live in a time where we are seeing many over promise and under deliver. We are attracted to quick fixes and promises of change, relief, or overnight shipping. This mentality often translates into our work and has been echoed by many other colleagues in other treatment settings. Treatment is not cheap. It usually stretches a family and becomes a real sacrifice for all involved, especially financially. We've sometimes noticed a comment like, "Isn't this what I am paying to fix?" or "I would expect for these behaviors to disappear soon enough with all this treatment and money being thrown around." This idea is expressed so often that we had to take measures to help readjust parent's expectations for change. The main sentiment in this type of attitude is to write a check and then check out. This is also gold-plating the onion.

FINAL THOUGHTS

By understanding your conditioning, how your loved one mirrors your conditioning, and the appropriate steps you can take to recognize and change, you can learn the deeper motives behind your subconscious and conscious behaviors, which are often rooted in pain avoidance.

We are limited in our ability to help you grow when you don't see how your past conditioning effects the way you behave, act towards others, and develop relationship tools. When a crisis hits and you experience emotional pain, the mentality quickly switches to, "I'm not broken, but you are." It's time to change that.

Until you can commit to the situation with a committed attitude, your money or time will go to waste, and you will head back where you started: going nowhere.

As you come full circle in your understanding of what personally fuels your actions, your awareness will now give way to more personal power to change your situation. Without this understanding, it's easy to fall into a default settings and patterns mode, which can create more distance between you and a struggling loved one.

REFLECTIVE POINTS & CORE PRINCIPLES TO REMEMBER:

- Your past conditioning as a child and young adult affects the way you resolve conflict and interact with your loved ones today.

- Your loved ones adopt your behaviors and adapt them to survive in their environment. Though they may alter them to fit their needs, they can easily be linked to your past conditioning in some way. By becoming more self-aware, you can change your behaviors and teach your loved ones tools to alter their negative patterns as well.

- When a relationship between two people is not healthy, both are at fault. If you are the parent/adult caretaker, you should be the first to assume responsibility. When you blame others and avoid looking at yourself as the problem, you are gold plating the onion.

Seven

DEFAULT SETTINGS & DEFAULT PATTERNS

I don't know enough about what's going on to really know what's really going on.

Several years ago, we remember stumbling across a YouTube video of author and philosopher David Foster Wallace who was invited to give a commencement speech to students at Kenyon College. It was so well received that it was published as a book called *This is Water*. The premise of the speech was on our responsibility as adults to exercise critical awareness of our certainties and ourselves because, as he says, "a huge amount of the things we feel totally certain about often turns out to be wrong and deluded."

Wallace continues, "Everything in my own immediate experience supports my deep belief that I am the absolute center of the universe, the realest most vivid important person in existence. We rarely talk about this natural basic self-centeredness because it's so socially repulsive, but it's pretty much the same for all of us. It is our default setting, hard wired into us at birth. Think about it, there's no experience that you've had that you are not at the absolute center of. The world as you experience it is there in front of you, or behind you. Other people's thoughts and feelings have to be communicated to YOU somehow, but your own are so immediate, urgent, real."[8]

If you watch the video you hear the audience chuckle when he talks

8. Sullivan, Jamie. "This Is Water - Full Version-David Foster Wallace Commencement Speech." YouTube. May 19, 2013. Accessed January 12, 2019. https://www.youtube.com/watch?v=8CrOL-ydFMI.

about our natural self-centeredness. They know, just like you and I do, that David is right. We often act from a place where the world revolves around our emotions, and we do it without even realizing it most of the time. This default setting can cause problems in our relationships because it gets in the way of our understanding. When we look at relational situations only from the view of where we stand, what we feel, and what we are experiencing, we forfeit the ability to understand what's real versus what we think is real because we are so totally involved in our own process. We only see what we want to see.

> Default Setting: The assumptions I make about life based on how I perceive it, which are self-centered in nature and often false (i.e., everyone is in my way, slowing me down, and getting under my skin).

Here's one example where our default settings as coaches got in the way of understanding:

> I remember not long ago speaking at length with a client about their addictions. He had given up some very hard substances. I was proud of him. Things were feeling really good. I was feeling proud of myself ... we were winning together it seemed! But then, over time, I noticed my client was becoming addicted to small things, insignificant things, like soda, video games, and cigarettes. I took it personally. All of the sudden, I felt attacked. I thought something was working, when it clearly wasn't. I was failing, I was upset with him, and I made assumptions. We started to talk and debate about his addictions. Sometimes things felt pretty heated, and I felt hopeless in my ability to help this person change the way I thought he needed to change. This was my default setting getting in the way, my ego, and my complete assurance that I was the healthy coach. What I was seeing with my client was truth! If he would just follow my lead, we could get somewhere.
>
> In other words, I was stuck on his addiction. I was acting from a place where Wallace so eloquently put it: "Other people's thoughts and feelings have to be communicated to YOU somehow," because yours are so very real and immediate. I'd have to say that my feelings even felt paramount to the success of our coaching work together. But, the reality was that my feelings weren't paramount in helping him recover, whereas his were.
>
> He knew exactly what was going on with him: he was totally overwhelmed socially. Without a beer in his hand or war stories about drugs, he felt alone, so he needed other sources to comfort him when he was being social. I was totally oblivious to this because I was still stuck on

what I felt he needed in order to heal. I was actually making things worse by fueling his thoughts of addiction and not allowing him to let them go. I couldn't step out of the tiny circle I drew around myself that said, "I'm okay to help, to be there for you, and to listen as long as I don't have to leave this circle (my beliefs about you and this situation). Don't make me step out of this circle!"

The moment I let go of what I thought was happening, accepted that I didn't know enough about what was going on to really know what was going on with my client—the moment I let go of my assumptions, and default settings—the healing and the insights came.

When we are totally certain about what we think is going on with our loved ones without removing ourselves from the equation, we often come to conclusions that are false and more about ourselves than our loved ones. We make assumptions, accusations, or judgments that can harm our relationships with others.

Here is another example where default settings can get in the way of our perceptions of people on a daily basis:

You are at the grocery store and the woman in front of you has a million coupons. She ensures the checker scans every coupon. You have a carton of milk and are totally annoyed with having to wait behind her. Your mind starts to think about all the ways she is holding you up, and you get even more annoyed (your default setting). You even go as far as to whisper under your breath, "Geez lady, you'll save like two bucks. I'll give you the money at this point."

She finally makes her way through the line and you pass her loading groceries into her car. You notice she's parked in a handicapped space and has a son in the back seat that appears to have cerebral palsy. You hear her excitedly tell her son that she saved $8.50, and she can finally buy him a new movie.

You feel guilty for looking at the lady as if she was just a penny pincher to be a penny pincher. You realize that your default setting betrayed you by making you see this woman as if she was being rude and thoughtless towards you. The truth? She wasn't purposely trying to slow you down. More than likely, she wasn't aware of you at all. She was probably just thinking about her son and the excitement she would see in his eyes when she told him they could afford to get something he wanted.

Do you see how quickly we can let our experience, our assumptions, or our default settings get in the way of how we view others? Can you imagine what this does to those we love and to our level of peace on a daily basis?

When Wallace talks about exercising some critical awareness, he's asking that we make a choice. We can either choose to go through our day believing that what we experience, feel, and believe is the absolute truth; that when we are hurt, offended, or stirred by someone through our interactions, it's about our pain, our anger, our justifications, our insecurities. The other option is to choose to be socially aware, to not let those basic instincts betray us and let our self-centered perspective clutter our ability to see things as they really are.

We have a saying that we like to keep in mind while consulting with clients: "We know very little about what's going on here to really know what's going on." It's a reminder that keeps our initial opinions and perceptions out of the equation until we have had enough time to be curious, ask questions, create different perspectives and possibilities, and to give the benefit of the doubt.

Here's a personal example where we were caught in a crossfire of wrongful assumptions, and where the benefit of doubt would have helped eliminate a lot of hurt feelings and discomfort.

Just the other day, I remember a friend was mad at me for not returning her calls or text messages. She had counted them up, knew exactly what time each message was left, and what they said in detail. She accused me of behavior that was "out of character," and she concluded in her mind (her default setting) that something was up with me and that I was being rude to her for a reason.

I remember feeling completely blindsided by this accusation of foul play, as I was thinking everything was cool between the two of us, and I didn't even remember half the calls or text messages she said she had sent. I honestly think to this day they are still lost in cyberspace. I was oblivious to how she felt, and she was wounded even further because it made her feel small, a feeling that made her remember her past.

I never wanted to make her feel small. Quite the opposite, I felt that I continually went to great lengths to show how much I cared about our friendship. Instead of trusting and believing in that truth, she was overtaken by her pain, her fears, and her negative thoughts. Her judgment was clouded and she began seeing other reasons as to why I may not have returned her call. From that negative thought, she reacted with a default pattern she had developed over the years to protect herself from feeling more emotional pain, which was to become withdrawn and passive aggressive.

When I acted completely stumped, questioning her reasoning behind such a conclusion, she also became defensive. The pattern deepened to protect her from more pain. Luckily, early on in my coaching career and conflict resolution trainings, I had come to understand that when others accuse us of doing certain things, they are instead feeling deeply guilty of doing those things themselves or would have done the same thing in the situation.

In this case, she was convinced that I was upset about something and therefore was ignoring her because that's exactly what she would have done if she was upset with someone. This is our default setting at work again, assuming that others react and experience things like we do, making it more about us. She assumed early on that if I was not returning her calls that I was clearly upset about something regarding our relationship, and she therefore created all sorts of untruthful conclusions in her mind. Meanwhile, I was on the other side of the world completely oblivious to her meltdown, distracted by everyday life, endless to-do lists, deadlines, and commitments.

I remember asking her, "What kept you from letting go of your default setting of assuming the worst in me when you felt wounded by my lack of response? What kept you from trusting that there were other possibilities that kept me from responding to you when you needed me to?" I remember saying, "It's not like I got up today and thought about how I was going to hurt or offend you, however, I'm being treated as if that is the case."

We often joke with clients when they are upset with those they love— the ones they seem to assume the worst about—that their husbands, wives, friends, or children must have gotten up that morning and said to themselves, "Today I'm going to do all I can to really upset you!"

Sounds crazy when you think about it that way, doesn't it? That's because, for the most part, it is. Most people don't wake up thinking about how they are going to make your life miserable. But somehow, as the day progresses, these thoughts become a part of your day and sometimes come with uncontrollable casualties. Emotions collide unintentionally, sparking old wounds or creating new ones that cause us to react as if it was all deliberate and intentional. We react before thinking because we are on the *me team*, and we then miss our opportunity to help each other grow through our daily mishaps.

For example, imagine you're a parent who has a son who will not find a job. It's frustrating to you because you know the importance of having a job. You quickly learn responsibility by going to work each day to earn money for your future. Maybe your default setting creates thoughts of failure because you feel as if you didn't motivate your son properly. Maybe you observe him playing video games and your default thought is that he's so lazy and it makes you feel angry, like he's taking advantage of you.

To stop feeling uncomfortable, you shift to a default pattern of constant nagging and guilt tripping to get him to move away from the TV and do something. This typically doesn't work as he talks back and walks out of the house upset. Notice that all of these thoughts so far have been about your experience, your fears, your perceptions, and nothing about his.

Maybe your son is overwhelmed with where to start looking for work and feels embarrassed to ask. He could be afraid that he can only get a customer service job and he has anxiety when people get angry with him. Until you consider these alternative possibilities outside of the circle of you, it's common to react in a way that could drive him away. Your understanding is totally unrelated to his experience. We have learned that when anyone comes from a place of thinking about only themselves, we invite the other person to respond in kind. It's like two semi trucks rolling towards each other on a one-lane highway, both intent on getting somewhere and each believing that driving on this highway is the most important thing they do. Nobody is willing to move over. But, if one semi truck doesn't get out of the way, they will collide and that collision could be disastrous.

So, who decides to pull over? Somebody needs to. We wish we lived in a world where both might be self aware enough to pull over and decide who should proceed, but most of the time, only one person needs to be selfless enough to step aside first, to reach beyond themselves and their perspective. This needs to be you. By doing so, you might see something you didn't before, like the oncoming semi has no brakes. You might also find that it is leaking fuel and needs to get to the nearest rest stop as soon as possible.

By stepping outside of your own default setting, you are better prepared to respond to others because you have conditioned yourself to gather more information and perspective before reacting and concluding incorrect things. Instead of pressing the accelerator full speed ahead, you can call for help. You can save not only yourself, but help the other person in need.

By letting go of your natural need to make things about you, you are open to seeing others. This can be beautiful in relationships. Everyone is seen, understood, and appreciated.

Before we move on to default patterns, you might have some further questions about how you can personally change. You may also wonder how you might be using default settings in a way that can be harming your relationships. We hope to address these questions at the end of this chapter, but for now, we ask you to journey into default patterns.

DEFAULT PATTERNS VERSUS DEFAULT SETTINGS

When we are using our default settings to regulate our thoughts, we will often find a pattern of action that validates the thoughts we have about others. These patterns have developed over time by observing others and how they deal in crises (i.e., family members who raised us or those we admire or respect). Almost always, the purpose of a default pattern is to provide relief from the emotional discomfort or pain felt from our thoughts or feelings about certain relationships or experiences with loved ones. These default patterns can also be due to situations where we are forced to experience unpleasant things because of others' actions. By falling into these patterns of reaction, we subconsciously try to prevent further pain and create quick fixes, while setting ourselves up for greater loss.

> Default Patterns: The behaviors I use to control and avoid discomfort or pain to justify my beliefs or my default settings.

Here's an example of where both default setting and patterns were used. Matthew's dad was always working and never home when things went wrong. Growing up, his mother was always the one putting out fires, it seemed. Now that he was a father with three teenagers, it felt as though the house was in constant chaos. When his wife would call him about the problems going on at home, he would think, *Not my department. Mom is supposed to deal with this sort of stuff.* He then would tell his wife that she would have to deal with things and would convince her that she was far more equipped than he was. He would then stay at work until he knew things would have died down at home, and he could return in peace.

This is a common pattern we've seen in fathers of families who are having problems. Do you recognize the default setting and pattern in this story? The default setting was the initial thought that he was being bothered by a problem that was not his … it was all about him at this point. His belief led him to feel that his wife was responsible for resolving issues at home while he was working hard for them.

Had he taken a moment to look outside of his discomfort and imagine what others might be going through—like the semi that pulls off the road—he might see that his responsibility as a father doesn't start and end at the office. His children want to connect with him, and his wife feels lonely balancing everybody's problems. In the end, he needed to realize that it was time to head home and be an equal partner in the emotional development of their teens. His default pattern to justify his default setting was to continue working longer than he needed so he didn't have to deal with the discomfort of conflict or deal with feeling inadequate with the current crises at home.

With our default settings and patterns, we can easily create an environment of justification. On a visit to a family we had been working with, we saw not only our own default settings and patterns, but those of this family. We were all out to dinner at a nice restaurant. They had really gone out of their way to make the experience nice and comfortable for us. We were sitting at a round table, in a fancy place, and things weren't going right. I started feeling stressed, responsible, and began analyzing the situation. I didn't want it to reflect badly on us that we couldn't do anything to make the situation better. Dad went stone cold, checked out, and didn't really hear what was happening. The kid we were coaching settled into an entitled fit and his mom's anxiety shot through the roof. Things got awkward fast.

Default settings and patterns had been on our minds and it suddenly became clear. It was like little name plates appeared in front of each us, labeling our default settings and we began acting the part. Somewhat emboldened, we began to express our thoughts on default settings and the patterns we were seeing in them. Dad being passive, Mom being anxious and overly invested, and the kid being entitled and pushing what boundaries he could.

I expected clarity, but received justification. I started hearing, "This is why I do this, and this I why I do that." Their settings had become patterns and were strengthened by their justifications. Once we saw ours at that table—our need to be right, to look good as coaches—we were able to stop and create a space where we were all able to see (probably for the first time) our settings and patterns, without the need for justification. We opened up to the family and showed them what we were seeing about ourselves, our patterns, and our default settings. We talked about our justifications or reasons for keeping the patterns alive. It was through the lens of us that they began to see their own patterns. Together, we began the process of understanding how their patterns have destroyed their family's ability to really communicate.

We have found that default patterns are just as destructive as default settings. Default patterns require action, not thoughts. It is our actions that are offensive and create negative responses with our loved ones. If we only experienced our default settings without acting, we would be the only ones injured.

When we coach at-risk youths and their family members, our first initial sessions are full of stories about how one person's actions have created a wedge between both parties. But, if we are to heal relationships, it makes sense that we (both the loved ones and their family members) have to be aware of the patterns that we use to create conflicts with loved ones and the thoughts that fuel our behavior.

The setting or the pattern is neither the chicken nor the egg; they go hand in hand. We start with recognizing default patterns first as they are the most obvious to corner, and then ask what thoughts fuel such behaviors (your default setting). If some of you are confused about what default patterns you might be using with loved ones, maybe you'll recognize yourself in the examples listed below. We make special note of these patterns as they seem to be very common in many people we work with. These patterns have driven many a wedge between loved ones.

THE PASSIVE DAD

This person has a hard time being involved when there is conflict going on at home. He either doesn't feel up to the task because he's overwhelmed with providing for his family, or doesn't feel like he has any suggestions to make the situation better. He decides mom is better suited for the job. He spends more hours in the office or does other things to contribute to his family in a positive way and makes himself feel better that way.

THE ANXIOUS MOM

The anxious mom is often times an antithesis to the passive dad. Since dad takes a back-seat role, mom has to overcompensate for the imbalance in the parenting relationship. She becomes someone who is overly anxious about anything her loved ones are doing. She becomes a sneak to try and reveal information and nags a lot. She overprotects to try to avoid any problems, even if it means preventing her loved ones from having healthy opportunities to fail and grow. In return, she teaches her loved ones to not trust themselves, and they develop that same anxiety about their lives in different ways. These feelings can present themselves in the following ways: "Nobody likes me at school, so therefore I feel anxiety every day I have to go to school." Or, "I'm not as good at sports as my brother, and I have anxiety about being a failure." Often times, this leads the loved one to find negative coping methods to try and heal the anxiety they feel, perpetuating the crisis even further.

THE DOUBTER

These are people that question every move their loved ones make. They have very little trust in their loved one's choices and behaviors, and they are unable to instill confidence in their loved ones. They help their loved ones avoid failure by ensuring success at all times. They make sure that their loved ones make all the right decisions and all the right connections, sometimes at the cost of others. This in turn creates painful scenarios for loved ones as they feel afraid to try new things. They are afraid of their own decisions. This creates low self-esteem and leads to negative coping methods of healing as well.

THE REALITY SHOW—DRAMA ADDICTS

One way of deflecting discomfort and pain is to create more drama. These people over-sensationalize or over-dramatize their lives and the lives of those they love. Minor conflicts and problems become a huge deal. They find that gossiping and getting involved in other people's problems is a natural practice. They don't feel normal if there isn't some type of crisis to be fixed or dealt with all the time. If there isn't a problem, their subconscious will somehow create a problem or they will fixate on other people's problems. They are often hypercritical of themselves, as well as their loved ones. If their loved ones refuse to play into the drama game or feed their stories and conversations, the parents often feel something is wrong. These parents can inadvertently ostracize their loved ones in different ways, making them feel as if they are alone or unwanted. One of their underlying addictions might also be the need to solve a problem all the time. If they can't be the hero, they feel like a failure. When they seek validation from their loved ones, they truly want to get sympathy. Through this method, they suck the life and power from others by always needing attention. This reflects a total lack of self-esteem and self-worth.

THE ENMESHED

These caretakers have a hard time understanding emotional boundaries with their loved ones. They seek to be constantly involved in their loved ones' lives, often using guilt or manipulation if the loved ones want to be alone or with other friends. They have a hard time separating caretaker and friend relationships and treat the loved ones as if they are adult friends the caretaker can confide in. They confuse their loved ones when they discipline them because the caretakers often see their loved ones above discipline. These caretakers have given their loved ones an adult-adult relationship, rather than the more appropriate caretaker-child relationship. Please note that we do believe in creating a friendship with your loved one and that having a friendship is essential to a healthy connection—as long as there are healthy boundaries. However, the enmeshed caretaker takes it a step further by crossing boundaries and discussing things that are not age appropriate for their loved ones, often involving them in personal aspects of the caretakers' lives that are personal or painful in order to get sympathy and relief. By forcing their loved ones to step past their experience as a child, the caretaker forces the children to help relieve their pain. This type of bonding can also create feelings of betrayal and pain in caretakers if the loved ones decide they want to be away from them.

THE OVERPROGRAMMER

These are parents that keep their children involved all the time because they fear what might happen to them if they don't. Please do not misunderstand us when we talk about overprogramming; we feel that it is very important to help your loved ones develop skills and talents that build a positive sense of self. Often, this healthy development of skills means being busy at lessons and so forth. Instead, we are talking about the parents who take it overboard. These are the ones that don't allow for any downtime—every moment needs to be calendared or scheduled. These are parents that compete with other parents and their children as they parade their loved one around, even when it's at their loved ones expense. This fantasy helps them to feel good about themselves as parents and people. By neglecting their loved ones' need to rest and regroup, they forfeit their loved ones' ability to practice building relationships with their peers, which often happens when one gets the time to relax and play. This neglect creates resentment between a loved one and a parent when forced to live at such an excessive speed.

THE BRIBER

To win favor from their loved ones, and to sometimes prevent feelings of discomfort, the bribers go out of their way to compensate for loss with bribes and gifts. If they've been away too long and feel guilty, they buy presents. They do this even when their loved one has been acting out negatively, just to gain control. They easily cave in and have weak boundaries. They find it easier to offer bribes than to stand their ground. They believe in giving their loved ones as many opportunities and things as they can, often trying to make up for the things they never had in their own lives. Often, they do this so much that they never give their loved ones the opportunity to learn hard work, dedication, failure, and success.

THE TALKER

This type of person has very little room for opinions other than their own. Instead of noticing when their loved one is checked out, they will continue to talk, and talk at them. They rarely give their loved ones an opportunity to share and feel, and if that rare moment comes, they often cut them off with negative feedback or explanations for why they shouldn't feel or act the way they do. They are convinced their intelligence is superior to others, and even when others are talking, they look for opportunities to trump the other person. Much of their self-esteem is wrapped up in the need to be acknowledged, respected, and heard—even if it's at the expense of their loved ones.

THE ROLLER COASTER

These types of people cannot commit to one thing, especially when it involves their loved ones. They sign them up for soccer, music lessons, or horseback riding, only to quickly fizzle out on attending when it becomes too difficult for them to maintain the schedule or motivate their loved ones. In other words, they ride high on the coaster with the excitement of trying new things, but then come crashing down when they realize hard work, commitment, and sacrifice is needed. Their loved ones receive the brunt of this and often become resentful and checked out when they realize there is very little follow through or support.

THE CONTROL FREAK

These types of caregivers typically try to control behaviors in their loved ones. They will control the clothes they wear, what they say, how they cut their hair, how long they talk on the phone, and where they go. They are constant nitpickers and naggers, trying to tweak and twist behavior to fit in the box they deem the safest and most suitable for their loved one. They are so wrapped up in the fear of failing themselves and those they love that they often can't see beyond their default and dysfunction. Failure is their kryptonite.

THE PERFECTIONIST

This person has a high level of internal criticism for themselves and for others, and they always expect high performances—especially from loved ones. Perfectionists like to use manipulation as a tool to make others feel guilt or shame for not performing as the perfectionists believed they were capable of. Sometimes, they will use threats to get the results they need. They are seduced by their life's truth: that if things become messy, faulty, or imperfect, it is because they weren't good enough or capable enough to pull it off. They are constantly finding fault in others when things go wrong. The perfectionist often has a strong control-freak default mode as well. Failure is also their kryptonite.

Though there are many other examples of default patterns that we didn't mention, did you notice anything that reminded you of yourself? If you didn't relate to any examples, take a moment to think about the times things have not gone well with your loved ones. How did you react? Is there something you say or do almost every time that creates more distance and misunderstanding? Are you passive, do you blame, do you walk away, or laugh at inappropriate times?

If you can pinpoint the pattern, you most definitely can get to the root of the pattern ... your thoughts or default setting. If you can change the thought to a more truthful thought by understanding and changing the way you react (your default pattern), you might see some better reactions and changes in those you love. If you aren't in a place where you are able to recognize these patterns, but you know they exist, it could be beneficial to talk to someone who can be honest with you about it. Ask them, "What kind of patterns do you see me falling into that cause problems in my relationships? How do you see me sabotage myself in relationships? How can I build healthier relationships with those I love?"

If you ask someone who can be honest with you, you should be prepared to receive what they have to offer without reacting. Try bringing a pen and paper with you, writing down what you hear, and not speaking or reacting at all to what they have to say. If you say anything, it should only be to ask questions about clarifying their point. You might want to do this with several people you can trust to see if there are similarities in their responses. The most important thing to focus on is recognizing what your destructive default patterns are, the thoughts that enforce them, how those thoughts impact your loved ones negatively, and the next steps to change them.

REFLECTIVE POINTS & CORE PRINCIPLES TO REMEMBER:

In order to make positive changes, we need to start developing a healthier default setting and healthier patterns. The examples we gave previously in this chapter may not mirror your current relationships. It is impossible for us to cover every possible situation as everyone is so different with unique home lives. But, it is our hope to give you some ideas to start recognizing thoughts and actions that are detrimental to relationships. Either way, it is your quest to dig deep and find things within yourself that could use some adjusting.

We know you will find the best way to move forward if you can remain open and honest in the process, even if it means bringing up painful memories or thoughts. It will take work. It will take practice and patience. You will need to be aware of your thoughts and behaviors. Remember, the goal is to change what is not working today. Here is a simple process we give our clients to help create a healthier way of coping with crises.

FILTER FACT VS BELIEF ACTIVITY

If your loved one does something that you think is completely stupid, hurtful, shameful, pain evoking, and uncomfortable, before you fall into your default pattern, take some time to regroup. How do you regroup? Here's a simple activity to help you.

Step 1

This activity was created to help you separate fact from feelings or beliefs. You can either take a mental note in your head or write what's happening on paper. The purpose is to help you take stock of what you really know about your current crises and what assumptions you are creating. It should look something like this:

The Facts	My Beliefs/Default Settings
My daughter came home late again.	I think she was getting high with her friends.
My daughter smells like alcohol.	My daughter is probably an alcoholic.
My daughter was out with her dead-beat boyfriend.	My daughter doesn't respect me and what I give her.

Notice how very little this parent knows about her loved one's current crisis, but also notice how deeply she feels about the situation. The new default requires you to filter information without a reaction, as often times we will react using accusations from our belief column, damaging relationships even more when our beliefs do not actually reflect the truth.

Step 2

Gain a different perspective. Before you come to any conclusion about the current crisis, remove yourself emotionally from this situation for some time. This could be an hour or a day. When you become detached, ask yourself, "What am I missing? What else could be going on?" Ask questions about those who may be involved in your current crisis, and get as much clarity as you can before you move forward.

Step 3

In addition to giving yourself enough time to disengage from your feelings, taking time to act means to also take time to think about how you will react. In order to not fall back into your default pattern, we ask that you do something different when you approach your loved one. Usually different is the antithesis of what you have already done. If you blame, find a way to take responsibility. If you react by invading private property and space, (i.e., journals, Facebook, phones, etc.) don't use that method. If you let things cool off, avoid it and never talk about it, create some time to engage in conversation. Exercise doing something different, healthier, and possibly more effective.

Step 4

As always, with any disagreement with loved ones, we strongly believe that you should involve your loved ones in the *what's next* process. Don't walk away from a disagreement until all parties' needs are met to the best of your ability.

Everyone—no matter what their current default setting and pattern is, no matter how they have reacted or responded to loved ones in the past—can make the choice to pause and say, "Maybe my loved one is going through something today, and I shouldn't automatically assume the worst. Maybe my loved one had no intention of harming me. They just might be struggling today."

When we stop and present ourselves with just one positive possibility, it changes our thoughts and our reactions. When we set aside our old assumptions, we are slower to judge, slower to jump to conclusions, and slower to react. We become more curious, more empathetic, and more thoughtful.

Now, say to yourself, "I'm willing to create another default setting and pattern. I'm willing to start listening in a different way, to put aside my assumptions, my expectations, and my original thought of what is happening to accept other possibilities."

It is in our willingness that we become hungrier to try, to take greater risks than we have before, and to connect in ways that were never before possible.

Eight
WHAT NOW?

"Repeat after me, my current situation is not my final destination."

—The Vibrant Mind

"It's a terrible thing, I think, in life to wait until you're ready. I have this feeling now that actually no one is ever ready to do anything. There is almost no such thing as ready. There is only now. And you may as well do it now. Generally speaking, now is as good of a time as any."

—Hugh Laurie

When loved ones experience a breakdown, there is a sadness that sets in, with moments of panic and desperation. Many caretakers will ask, "What now? What can I do that will provide the most effective support for my loved one to reverse the downward tailspin they are in?"

The tailspin will take a myriad of things to stop it. The web of a breakdown is sticky and a loved one's breakdown has many strongly-developed and complicated layers. It could take treatment, therapy, medications, or everything. You will know more in time as you uncover the layers of their pain and dysfunction. You will also know more as you uncover the layers of your patterns, settings, and pain. It will most certainly take time, and it will undoubtedly take change within you. You will have to change the way you work and relate with your loved one. You are the cornerstone of their existence and support.

Without things changing at home, loved ones will most likely fall back into their own default settings and patterns. This is a waste of time and money for anyone dealing with a loved one who is struggling. The most important thing you can do for them is to work on changing the way you relate to your loved one, in addition to figuring out which treatment or resolution plans might be best.

What now then? You can begin with this series of questions:

- If your loved one is going through a breakdown, how are you a co-creator?
- What are you committed to change in your own life in order to connect with your loved one?
- What kind of conversations are you willing to have with your loved one based on the information you now know?
- What apologies need to be made? How would they react to this apology and what doors would open?
- What boundaries need to be fixed?
- What does my loved one need from me most right now? Who do they need me to be?
- What part of this book stung the most and what did I learn from this pain? (Often what hurts most is where your work should begin.)

We want you to take some time—even though you might feel like there is no time in your current crisis—to work on what we talked about in the previous chapters and these questions. Don't read this book one time and find yourself enlightened and fixed. Go back and read it again. Deepen your understanding. Catch things you might have missed. Read with the intention that you are going to answer all questions honestly. Take some time to think on the reflective points. Use a journal and do some soul searching in each chapter. Ask your mind questions about how and what needs to change. Write down the things that come to you as inspiration, and then put in place an action plan to do something different, something better for you and a loved one.

When solving problems, most of our inspiration doesn't come at the exact moment we are seeking inspiration, but more during the times we find ourselves open to letting our minds wander. This could be in the shower, listening to music, or riding a bike. We try and have something close to write thoughts down when the inspiration comes. We also try and create moments where we are free from distractions, like a phone, TV, or kids.

Next, be patient with yourself during this process. You can't change your behaviors overnight just by reading. You need to practice, have productive conversations about these topics, try and fail, and try again until you succeed. You need to learn new default settings and implement new ways of thinking and reacting. You became who you are over many years of practice and conditioning. Though it doesn't have to take years to change, allow yourself some time and space to change.

You need to find a coach, therapist, or trusted ally who can help you see things differently. Find someone you can be real and honest with and someone you can trust will treat you with honesty. Don't allow yourself to be disillusioned by someone who will say things they think you want to hear. We know it's painful to accept responsibility. That will never change. You can, however, change your attitude and willingness to accept that you aren't perfect.

> When our child was living away from home for rehabilitation, we were going through counseling at the same time with his counselor. At first, I thought the sessions were going to be about informing us about how he was doing. I quickly learned that the sessions were going to be nothing about that and more about me. This was really hard to stomach at first. I didn't want to accept that I needed help. I was resistant. But then my eyes were opened, and my guard was dropped. I was finally understanding how I was contributing to my loved one's breakdown, how I was a co-creator. If it wasn't for the deepest love I had for my son, I don't know that I would have been willing to do the work. Thankfully, I had that awakening. Many people I've come across in similar situations aren't ready to change. They ask for my advice mostly because they just want to talk to someone, not because they want to do anything about it. It makes me sad to see that they were unable to make headway. If only they were willing to accept some difficult truths.
>
> —Martha

> It was hard practicing new ways of dealing with my loved one. I was reluctant and hopeless that anything would change, but then miraculously, little by little, things changed. I was changing in a better way. I wasn't as upset or angry and I had a better grasp on what was going on. It didn't always mean that my loved one made the right choices—though they were trying too—but I was in a much better place to deal with what they were going through than I ever had been before.
>
> —David

If we can teach you to be more resilient, flexible, and open in the way you react to an at-risk loved one, you will be more prepared to take an even deeper look into the way you resolve conflict.

A QUICK ASIDE:

You may be thinking, "Wait! What have you left me with here?"

We've left you with a choice. This process of reconnection begins with you as the caretaker, as the one who has the best chance at starting things anew with your at-risk loved one. We leave you with a choice: to truly take our advice, sit down with yourself, and find your bearings amidst all the pain and suffering around you or to step away from the process of healing. Can you ask yourself the introspective questions we have peppered throughout this whole book?

This first book is about you, your pains, your struggles, your patterns and settings, all things that keep you from truly connecting. We wrote this book because we know that before resolving any conflict, you need to check your own foundation. You need to be ready to own your part of your current conflicts. You need to understand your triggers and settings so when you truly jump in to resolve your current realities, you do so on your best foot and with the right intentions. All of that takes time. It takes bravery. It takes patience.

In the meantime, if you have further questions, or need more coaching while you take this journey, you can interact with us online at BangHeadHere.com.

DEDICATION

My family first: thanks to my inspiring parents and supportive sisters, and my three rockstar grandmas who taught me to dream big. To my boys, Carlos and Ivan, who have taught me the reciprocal nature of connection. You are becoming great men. For Charissa Adelmann, my coach extraordinaire, who never gave up on keeping me connected to what's important. And to all my clients whose late-night phone calls and trust have taught me that connection isn't easy, but is ultimately worth it.

I am grateful to be your connection ally.

—Josh

To my parents: at our darkest moments, we had the courage to stand up to the mirror and embrace change. To the teens who remind me that their unique voice needs to be appreciated and heard especially in moments when they are struggling the most. For all of my friends and clients who've trusted me with their stories when it was difficult to tell them.

I am grateful to be your connection ally.

—Hollie

For Hannah Rushton who, as an editor and coach, has guided us through the process of publication and has believed in the vision of this book. To Heidi Helm, for the book cover design. And to all of our friends and family members who reviewed manuscript after manuscript and stuck with us. Thank you!

We are grateful to be your connection ally.

—Hollie and Josh

ABOUT THE AUTHORS

Josh Brazier

As written by his co-author, Hollie Henderson.

Josh and I grew up approximately ten miles away from each other. Though our interaction during our teen years was sparse, our mutual relationships and connections to home and friends would later bring us together in our young adult years. After our college years, I learned that Josh had started his own non-profit organization called Kaiizen, which served a small Mexican orphanage in Ensenada.

Ironically, I too was involved in non-profit work at the time, teaching high school and college students about dating violence prevention, and healthy relationship development. It was a relief to be able to talk to someone who understood the hardships of many we worked with. Josh showed incredible empathy and dedication to the cause of doing good for others. I thought his love for helping and mentoring children and adults was admirable.

His passion helped him align with others to foster growth in his company. Kaiizen soon grew to serve not only Mexican orphanages, but those in Swaziland, India, Brazil, Zambia, and Peru. A couple of years after we connected, I learned he was not only running Kaiizen, but working with at-risk boys in a teen-rehab facility. He had used his love of travel and philanthropy to offer a special mentoring opportunity for boys who were often self absorbed and lost in their own struggle, hoping to expose them to the incredible medicine of service. While personally mentoring them and exposing them to beautiful and unique parts of the world, the boys' lives changed. I joined him on one of his trips and became part of the incredible organization he had created.

I loved Josh's easy-going attitude, his ability to connect to these boys, and his deep commitment for the organizations he served. There are very few people who can handle the stress of managing a group of at-risk youths—many of which are coming off detox programs and who are sometimes highly medicated—while creating something of meaning and purpose for them. It makes him and his insights one of a kind and extremely valuable.

Over the last fifteen years, he has honed his skills and intuition to know what really works for people who are struggling. He has practiced, failed, and succeeded more with all different types of personalities. It is through that experience that I know what he has to teach others really can and does work.

He has taught me many things over the course of writing this book. His unique insights have often lifted me and my perspective in how I approach individuals to teach certain concepts. He is an explorer, an avid studier and reader, and an incredible storyteller.

He allows you to be in your own space and walk with you there, a gift to many looking for compassion on their own journey. He is passionate about connection and is a true connection ally; it is why so many call him friend and mentor, and why many are willing to give up their time and resources. They follow him into areas that are challenging and measurably less comfortable than their every day lives.

People love his quest to bring everyone together, to give them the tools they need to feel bonded and connected to each other, in hopes those bonds will help as make their lives a greater success. He always asks, "Have you read this book?" as he hopes to lift you higher, so all who are surrounded by him feel that they can be taken to new places of learning and understanding. He does not boast his own accomplishments. If you succeed, he succeeds. His courage to try over and over again with no guarantee for success has drawn me towards his work and his cause.

Hollie Henderson

As written by her co-author, Josh Brazier.

I remember being at Hollie's house one night with a bunch of friends. We had all gathered to support her. She was about to take a big leap. There was a lot of energy in the room as Hollie outlined her dream. Music is Hollie's passion. She felt it was time to make that announcement to the world.

As she outlined her plan for a concert, we all realized this wasn't going to be a show at some small venue—a "testing the waters" type deal. Hollie was, in fact, renting out the biggest venue in our area and she was planning to fill it—with our help. There was no doubt in her plans, as Hollie is tenacious and passionate. Music draws people to her and she excels with people.

She organized all of us into a team and soon we were out selling hundreds of tickets. Like I said, it was a huge leap of faith. Luckily, things like that don't phase Hollie.

The concert was a huge success and she rocked a full house. Soon after, I left to go to college out of state and we fell out of touch. Fast forward many years and we find ourselves eating lunch and catching up. After realizing how similar our paths had been and voicing some frustrations, this book was born.

Over the course of writing, I came to see who Hollie had become through her experiences and why she is such a master coach. You see musicians write to connect with people; we all know that. But Hollie began to see how to extend her inspiration beyond her music and fans. I think she started to get involved in coaching on a deeper level because she saw the needs of people were overwhelming.

Starting off as camp counselor exposed her to the power of connection and the ability to have influence with a captive audience. She'd use her dreams about music to inspire the girls she worked with there. When you work with youth, you begin to see patterns. Hollie picked up on one of those patterns among the girls and women she helped and coached. She saw that dating and violence went hand in hand in the areas she worked. After seeing the amount of pain and damage abuse created, she took to the stage again.

She created a curriculum and presentation to help educate and stop the proliferation of violence and abuse towards women, and men. She traveled around to give her message to venues including shelters, correctional facilities, schools, and colleges. As she found her voice for those who were voiceless, she began to coach.

Over the years, Hollie has coached many out of difficult situations. She is open and honest with her struggles as a teen and an adult, which only adds to her legitimacy with those she mentors. Whether working in a shelter for battered women or throwing a benefit concert to raise awareness about issues she is passionate about, Hollie gives strength to those who have none. Whether she is coaching or giving a class on how to turn your passions into reality, Hollie's voice gives hope to those still struggling to find their own.

I am someone she's given a voice to. As she and I labored over the concepts in this book, she has pushed me to find what really works. She's challenged me on things, as an exercise to see if I really believed in my theories. She helped me hone my coaching skills. She's given me confidence in my life's work and I am indebted to her.

Recently, I had the chance to watch her speak to an audience of women who have suffered. The ladies were so attentive, hanging on her words. Her presentation was clear, concise, and compelling. She is connected to human nature in a very organic and enviable way. People want to hear what she has to say.

I hope you get the chance to meet Hollie one day. I hope you get the chance to settle into the kind of conversation where you know you are her focus. A safe place where you say things you never thought you'd say. Where all of your thoughts fall on trusted ears and a compassionate heart.

Hollie is the coach she is, the person she is, the rock star she is because no matter what life threw at her, she'd still have the guts to get up on stage and sing about it, all the while inspiring you to do the same. Hollie is a hero of mine and I know to many others. Keep rocking, Hollie.

INDEX